Contents

Teaching In Troubled Times

Kathy Paterson

Pembroke Publishers Limited

© 2010 Pembroke Publishers
538 Hood Road
Markham, Ontario, Canada L3R 3K9
www.pembrokepublishers.com

Distributed in the U.S. by Stenhouse Publishers
480 Congress Street
Portland, ME 04101
www.stenhouse.com

We acknowledge the financial support of the Government of Canada through the Book
Publishing Industry Development Program (BPIDP) for our publishing activities.

We acknowledge the assistance of the Government of Ontario through the Ontario
Media Development Corporation's Ontario Book Initiative.

Library and Archives Canada Cataloguing in Publication

Paterson, Kathy
    Teaching in troubled times / Kathy Paterson.

Includes index.
ISBN 978-1-55138-254-8

1. Teaching. 2. Teacher effectiveness. I. Title.

LB1025.3.P3852 2010   371.102   C2010-903825-8

Editor: Kate Revington
Content Review: Ardis Kamra
Cover Design: John Zehethofer
Typesetting: Jay Tee Graphics Ltd.

Printed and bound in Canada
9 8 7 6 5 4 3 2 1

Preface

Before I dwell for more than a hundred pages on the troubles of our world today, let me say that, overall, life is amazing, wonderful, and beautiful. We are a society with more wealth, health, and longevity than ever before. We have, it seems, every luxury imaginable, better health management, and generally more fun than our ancestors. This book takes a gloomy stance only so that it can offer hope. Its goal is to help teachers find the joy, the beauty, and the fun of their profession despite the media-fanned troubles always in their faces.

Teaching in Troubled Times begins with an exploration of fear which underlies all of the troubles experienced by students, teachers, and parents. Chapter 1 clarifies this often difficult-to-define feeling and provides teachers with concrete ways to help students handle it. It finishes with a section called Spontaneous Support, which presents a strategy that with minor changes will be used throughout the book.

The rest of the book is composed of the following chapters:

- Concerning the World (Chapter 2)
- Concerning Children of the New Decade (Chapter 3)
- Concerning Parents Today (Chapter 4)
- Concerning New-Age Teachers (Chapter 5)
- Concerning Schools in 2010 and Beyond (Chapter 6)

Although chapters differ in length, each contains similar structures. Each provides an explanation of the specific "trouble" and general concerns related to that area and their impact on teaching. Each provides background as well as ideas, strategies, tips, and recommendations to assist teachers in addressing the trouble.

Formula Fives consist of five helpful practices, steps, or ideas that can be shared with students or parents, or used as teacher background. The initial charts are short; they permit quick access and easy recall of pertinent ideas. The Formula Five elaborations represent classroom strategies combined with teaching tips and can be readily found by scanning the Contents.

Good Idea notes are quick suggestions to increase the effectiveness of a task or situation. They appear in margins adjacent to pertinent information; however, teachers can use them anywhere at any time.

Within some sections are Motivators — quick, to-the-point games, activities, and tasks that the teacher may adopt to "get kids interested." Since the motivators are intended to be used as "teacher tools," most appear in Chapter 5.

Good Reads identify picture books or, in some cases, young adult chapter books pertinent to the areas under discussion. It is important to remember that picture books work equally well with students of all ages.

The Introduction explains how this book came to be written.

Introduction: Finding Fun and Joy in Bleak Times

Not long ago, a teacher asked me how she was supposed to teach her students *anything* in days such as these. When I encouraged her to explain what she meant, she pointed out that the world around us is in chaos and that children are inundated with stories of tragedies, floods, fires, plagues, famine, homicides, crashes, accidents, crimes, poverty, and lack of personal safety. We live in a perpetual state of fear, she said. How, she questioned, could she help the children she teaches to grow, develop, and become, or remain, optimistic about education, learning, and even about themselves in the face of the many disasters, dangers, and terrors all around them? Was it possible, she queried, to teach students courage and independence when parents, justifiably afraid for their children's safety, *over*protect them? Often, even elementary schools, she pointed out, have resident police officers — a sign of perceived danger. Or what about the exhausted and often frightened parents who struggle with job loss, debts, or divorce and perhaps neglect their children and fail to notice that they, too, are suffering from anxieties? Then, she added, there are sometimes great problems with school shortages, especially in our struggling economy that seems to overlook the enormous financial requirements of a good education. How could she teach without enough books or supplies? How, she wondered, could she motivate kids for learning when she constantly had to "make do" in the classroom, and then go home and "make-do" all over again because her husband had recently lost his job and her salary alone was insufficient to support her family . . .

"It's all so terribly troublesome," she said with a sigh. "How can I have any positive influence on the kids when all around them their very existence, their future, looks so bleak? I feel helpless." Finally, she asked, "What's the point?"

Occasions a Good Teacher Would Not Miss

I found this last comment the most upsetting. Yes, the twenty-first century seems to be fraught with troubles and children are not immune from them. Yes, these troubles make teaching more difficult, more challenging, more exhausting. But yes, there *is* a point! A definite point! Teachers can, and will, make a difference in children's lives, regardless of what is going on all around them. It is important that teachers stand firm in their belief that their work makes a difference and that they instruct with courage and passion. As U.S. philosopher Ralph Waldo Emerson put it: "Bad times have scientific value. These are the occasions a good learner would not miss." I believe that bad times are occasions a good *teacher* would not miss.

Our students are caught in the tangle of world unrest. Daily, they are faced with the resulting stress and despair. Immersed in technology as they are, they cannot escape the strong visual and auditory messages of our troubled times. And, of course, there's the "gadgetry pandemic." The past decade has seen a plethora of constantly changing gadgets — one month's gadget is obsolete the next. Who can keep up? And how does this affect education and teaching?

Beyond these currents, children still face the typical challenges of childhood, such as teasing, rejection, self-doubt, fear, and less-than-perfect role models. These obstacles to growth and development don't go away just because the world is throwing bigger, messier, scarier problems at them. Instead, these problems tend to intensify as youngsters suffer the pressures of family and ultimately, world unrest, acting-out more frequently and with more passion towards their environment.

It seems today's students suffer a triple dose of nastiness: from the world, from their peers, and from themselves; yet if they are to evolve into successful adults, they must *learn* to deal with and ultimately, overcome, the problems in their existence. The operative word is "learn," which leads to school and to teachers. How, then, can teachers push past these negative influences, these ever-present reminders of humankind's failures, and reach and teach their students? What can they teach that will help their students survive? Can teachers and the educational messages they wish to deliver be more important than life's horrific realities? I believe they can — and they must. I believe that teachers can be the key forces in creating better futures for their students. They must be, for as John W. Whitehead, author of *The Stealing of America*, puts it: "Children are the messages we send to a time we will not see."

The Power of Positive Teaching

As teachers, we cannot change the world our students see today or will see tomorrow, but we can influence how they deal with both, with the hope that they will be smarter than we were and will exist more cooperatively, more fruitfully, and with more confidence and wisdom than we did. That is an ambitious statement — a grand hope. But I am convinced that the power of positive teaching, especially now, will be the cornerstone of a better tomorrow for our students. I also believe that all good teachers feel exactly the same way and may, therefore, be seeking ways to empower their teaching, to motivate their students in spite of less-than-perfect situations, and to make the best choices about what to teach, how to teach, and when to teach. The situation may be less than perfect, but all the amazing teachers out there still want to be the best teachers possible and are seeking anything that will help. I hope that this book will be of help to all those amazing teachers and their amazing students, and will facilitate their mutual transition through these troubled times.

Balancing Child Fears and Teacher Stresses

Teaching in Troubled Times is based on four premises and strives to achieve a balance between them.

- First, teachers are busy, overworked individuals who are concerned with the welfare of their students.
- Second, when a child has serious worries, questions, or fears, teachers want to be comfortable with how and when to step in, how much assistance to offer, and what techniques or strategies work.

- Third, our world is a world in chaos, where fear runs rampant — children are affected by that.
- Fourth, for teachers seeking the best possible ways to help their students handle concerns and fears, there is *far* too much information available.

Together, these four premises create a problem for teachers: a problem of needing to quickly identify and correctly choose the information that will benefit the majority of their students in a rapidly changing world.

One obvious dilemma these educators face is how to select from the overwhelming amount of information in articles, books, newspapers, magazines, and on the Internet, as well as on television talk shows and self-help shows, the golden nuggets that teachers need. It seems that everyone has a suggestion for helping our students, but most of the suggestions are lengthy; time consuming to read, understand, and implement; and perhaps premised on much teacher studying and preplanning, not to mention hours of initial researching. *Teaching in Troubled Times* seeks to expedite the process, to provide quick, easy-to-use, and effective strategies that teachers can use on the spot as needed. It is based on the appreciation that there are steps and procedures for dealing effectively with a variety of specific student concerns, many of which are based on aspects of our current troubled times, including war, terrorism, disease, and natural disasters.

When a child asks a question about or related to one of these matters, the teacher *must* answer. Teachers are considered to be experts, to "know everything" (at least by their students). So, when a child approaches a teacher with questions or worries about a world trouble, the best guess is that the child is concerned, maybe even anxious, most probably for his or her own safety and the safety of loved ones — *not* a situation that can be put off. At the least, the teacher must acknowledge the concern, reassure the child, and promise to return to it in more detail at a set time. "You are worried about the flu epidemic and I can understand why. I'm worried too, but it's good to know that health officials are working hard to control it. We'll talk about it more in period 3 today." As soon as possible thereafter, use the Formula Five: Spontaneous Support Strategy (see pages 23–24). This strategy relies on the teacher being honest with the child and telling the truth about the troubling situation.

Troubles That Have an Impact on Teaching

For purposes of this book, it was necessary to narrow "troubles," concerns, or areas of difficulty, depending on how you want to view problematic situations, from a never-ending list. I asked teachers for guidance, using questions such as these:

- "What troubles specific to the world today interfere with your teaching?"
- "How is teaching in 2010 different from and possibly more difficult than teaching 10 or 20 years ago?"
- "In what ways do world situations, crises, or difficulties affect your classroom instruction *differently* today than in the past?"

Their responses were varied, but I was able to compile them into the following list from which I based the content of *Teaching in Troubled Times*. At the end of each the most relevant chapter(s) are identified.

- Many kids are worried about world problems. They often talk endlessly about catastrophic situations and fret about how they might be affected. Even the youngest kids, many of whose parents try to shield them by restricting television, for example, are affected negatively by interactions with peers whose viewing is less restricted. (Chapter 2)

- Many kids (particularly older ones) feel helpless in the face of overwhelming world issues and often adopt a "why bother" attitude. (Chapters 2 and 3)
- The whole fear attitude of living today, promoted and heightened by the media, causes tension for adults and children alike. (Chapter 1)
- Some students are addicted to modern gadgets, while other students don't even have them. This difference not only widens the gap between haves and have-nots, but puts further stress on teachers who have to find ways to make routine lessons more exciting than current gadgets. (Chapter 5)
- Rapid changes in family dynamics and demographics are directly affecting children. (Chapter 4)
- Many parents fighting to survive job loss, separation, divorce, or financial desperation are less able to be supportive of their children. (Chapter 4)
- There are more single-parent families than ever before. In itself this situation is not problematic, but the effect of a weaker economy on single parents, and hence on the children, is more devastating. (Chapters 4 and 6)
- Many of today's parents either overprotect or leave their offspring alone, with negative results. Children may be overprotected due to fear for their personal safety (from predators, kidnappers, and so on) or left alone because parents have to work hard to meet financial obligations. In both situations, children may become less confident and independent, less able to problem-solve, less resilient to negative situations, and more fearful overall. (Chapter 3)
- Parents, disturbed by these negative behaviors in their offspring, are turning more frequently to teachers to seek help for their children — and teachers do not necessarily have answers. (Chapter 5)
- Many kids today don't seem to know who they are, what they want, where they are headed or why. For whatever reason, including perhaps too little emphasis on or time for self-discovery, they appear to be lacking a sense of self. (Chapter 3)
- Kids today are inundated with media violence and horror. The whole issue of access to any and all information on the Internet is problematic. (Chapter 2)
- Overall, social skills in children appear to be waning, at least in part, teachers believe, to the overuse of individually played computer games and similar solitary activities. (Chapter 3)
- The fear of failure has grown to the point where many students will do almost anything to avoid failure. Some of their behaviors appear positive — for example, studying harder — but a closer look at them may prove otherwise. (Chapter 1)
- There appears to be more covert bullying in today's classrooms possibly because kids in negative home situations are becoming more clandestine at taking out their anxieties on others (e.g., shunning, name-calling, ostracizing, and framing) or because of the growth of cyber-bullying. The National Crime Prevention Council's definition of cyber-bullying is "when the Internet, cell phones or other devices are used to send or post text or images intended to hurt or embarrass another person." A Canadian study (Wiki.ucalgary.ca) conducted in 2008 states that cyber-bullying has doubled in the past 10 years. Research from the Australian Department of Education (2007) suggests that "covert bullying has the potential to result in more severe psychological, social and mental health harm than overt bullying, and also has the capacity to

inflict social isolation on a much broader scale." Some teachers even feel that covert bullying may lead to more physical-abuse types of bullying. (Chapter 3)

- Many of today's kids are not motivated to learn basics, especially if they cannot use technology. Classroom "seatwork" is considered boring, mundane, and time wasting, which makes teaching basic skills more difficult. (Chapter 5)
- The whole issue of fitness, together with childhood obesity, is troubling for teachers who are expected to teach to this concern and deal with it appropriately in the classroom. (Chapter 3)
- Teachers, swamped with curriculum that seems impossible to meet, often wonder why they are in the profession and what their personal and professional goals are. Their uncertainty is aggravated by the unsettled state of the world. (Chapter 5)
- Schools are not keeping up — there are shortages of books, equipment, and supplies. The failing economy is making this situation worse. (Chapter 6)
- The world is changing so rapidly that reference-type materials are often outdated before they are paid for. Many schools cannot keep pace, and unlike former times when parents might have been expected to fund-raise for texts or to pay "specialty fees" for Art, Drama, and Science, they can no longer be expected to do so. (Chapter 6)

This is a lengthy list. Teachers will likely find themselves nodding in agreement with at least some of the entries. If so, they can locate those areas in the book and expect to find suggestions. First, though, Chapter 1 addresses the response most often aroused by a consideration of the many troubles in the world: fear.

CHAPTER 1

Concerning Fear

Fear, an uncomfortable emotion experienced by us all, appears to be prevalent and problematic in today's world. I have heard it said that we live in a *culture* of fear. "Security" has become a buzz word, "Big Brother" is watching, and advertisers are marketing fear aggressively. Most certainly, the whole fear culture is promoted and glamorized by the media, which, in turn, are more influential than ever due to rapid advancements in technology. There we have the formula for fear: media tall tales, cameras literally everywhere (even in tiny convenience stores), and overly available technology all combining to create discomfort and upset for our students. Why? Financial gain. Fear sells.

The effect of this unhappy situation on teaching is readily apparent. Children are afraid, and teachers must not only understand how to assist their students in overcoming or handling their fears, but also know how to deal with the immediate repercussions of fears, both small and extreme.

In his amazing book *Risk: The Science and Politics of Fear*, Dan Gardner refers to two kinds of fear. "Reasonable fear" is constructive and encourages attention to the task or situation at hand, such as when fear of snakes forces us to flee from a venomous bite; "unreasoning fear" forces us to make foolish decisions that are counterproductive to effective living. An example of an unreasoning fear would be the obsessive washing of hands to prevent disease contagion. Handwashing is effective, but the compulsive racing for soap and water represents an unreasoning fear and may even have negative side effects. Another example of an unreasoning fear in children would be the fear to go outside in case terrorists are lurking. Again, although caution around strangers and the taking of appropriate safety measures are important, the complete isolation of a child as a result of this fear makes it unreasoning and almost debilitating. Paranoia, of course, is an unreasoning fear at its worst, and its severity demands intervention by a psychology professional; it will not be discussed in this book. The unreasoning fears in children — in fact, in all of us — are incapacitating and can cause unnecessary pain and suffering if not dealt with appropriately. Teachers must deal with both reasonable and unreasoning fears in their classrooms.

Teachers must also deal with group fear. Children are vulnerable. They are easily led. Consequently, if one or two of them express a fear, suddenly an entire group is sharing that fear, whether it is valid or not. At this point, the teacher must step in and take charge so that the group fear does not escalate — we are all familiar with the concept of mob hysteria.

One final fear will be discussed: fear of failure. True, this is not *just* a current fear, but it seems to have spiked in today's troubled times. It is so problematic in classrooms that it bears mentioning.

Basically, then, the teacher is first responsible for determining the nature of a fear. Is it little or big? Is it reasonable or unreasoning? Is it a single child's fear or a group fear? Is it a fear of failure? All such questions must be answered before the teacher intervenes. Doing this can be a daunting task, but teachers are noted for successfully undertaking daunting tasks.

H. P. Lovecraft, an author of horror, fantasy, and science fiction, stated, "The oldest and strongest emotion of mankind is fear." I believe that statement continues to be as true today as it was in the first part of the twentieth century when Lovecraft wrote. Fear grows in darkness, multiplies with ignorance, and accelerates with reinforcement. It can be a child's nemesis and a teacher's nightmare. If a child is afraid of something even as small as walking alone to the washroom, the teacher has to deal with the fear before any manner of teaching can begin. How can that be done most effectively? The text that follows aims to provide concise, constructive ideas.

Reasonable Fears

Some fears are valid and reasonable. They are based on the perception of risk, and where children are concerned, that risk is personal and immediate. There are little fears, such as the fears of overstepping boundaries, of upsetting someone, of being seen as a fool, of being teased, of being mediocre. There are bigger fears, such as the fears of losing a loved one, of war, of disease, of terrorist attacks. All of these are reasonable fears based on real situations. A child's fear of dogs might be based on once being bitten by a dog. The existing reasonable fear prompts him to move safely away from a barking dog. As such, it serves to protect him. Teachers are well aware of reasonable fears in their students — students are usually quite willing to voice them. Reasonable fears often revealed in the classroom include fear of ridicule or ostracism by peers, fear of failure, fear of embarrassment, and, of course, fear of bullies. The teacher can recognize these fears by watching and listening when children interact, and by asking pertinent questions if a particular fear is suspected. These fears may appear to be "small," but to the child, they are anything but. Using the Formula Five offered in this section is recommended.

Unreasoning Fears

These fears tend to result from the big, scary, "today-based" troubles that children are subject to in our modern world, and unfortunately, they are lurking in classrooms everywhere. What makes them unreasoning is not that they are false, but that somehow the risk perception associated with them has become skewed, generating disproportionate fear and consequent disproportionate behaviors. For example, if even the sight of a dog on television caused fear in a child, that would be an unreasoning fear.

An unreasoning fear is based on two concepts: (1) if someone believes that something can happen and (2) if that something is possible. In other words, if a child truly believes that bullies at school will physically hurt him at recess, the fear associated with this belief can quickly become unreasoning to the point where the child is terrified to enter *any* school *any* time, even when accompanied by an adult.

The media frenzy associated with any traumatic event, such as 9-11, is largely responsible for unreasoning fears. And our children, unfortunately, are not exempt from their messages. Although tragic and horrific events, such as 9-11, certainly promote fear, the media's constant replaying of them is what creates *unreasoning* fears. For example, almost 10 years after 9-11, I happened upon a television news show that reviewed the catastrophe in horrendous detail. Children not even born at the time could now witness all the gory details. Media blitz was, in this case, helping to create unreasoning fears for personal safety in children. Young people might come to fear terrorist activity in their own cities or towns.

For some children, this fear is almost debilitating. An example would be Sue, the Grade 4 student who was afraid to venture outside at recess. "The terrorists have nukes," she told her teacher. "I heard my grandpa say that. They could nuke us whenever they wanted to." Of course, this is not a realistic threat but for Sue, it was real; it was an unreasoning fear that prevented her from behaving in a normal manner.

School-aged children express other unreasoning fears: fears of violence, fears of sexual abuse, rape, or abduction, fears of war, fears of diseases and plagues, fears of famine and extreme poverty, and fears of natural disasters. All of these possible risk situations are sensationalized by the media. To reiterate, because of advancements in technology today, children are exposed to many catastrophic situations; unfortunately, many youngsters have developed unreasoning fears related to them.

Teachers will quickly recognize these unreasoning fears because children will talk about them and may display erratic behaviors. For example, a child could refuse to play on the playground because she believes a pedophile is waiting there even though the area is well secured and policed by adults, or, like Sue, a child could be afraid to leave the school at all.

Teachers must take constructive action against fears. Part of this is talking to the parents or guardians, but the teacher can also take actions in class, too. One good strategy that can be used with both reasonable and unreasoning fears is outlined by the following Formula Five. The goal is not to minimize the fears but to help children recognize the unreasoning ones and find ways to deal effectively with either kind of fear. This Formula Five can be used successfully with individuals or with a whole class.

Invite verbalization and questions.
Self-disclose using "I" statements.
Be honest.
Focus on the positive.
Create an action plan.

Formula Five: Helping Children Deal with Fear

Invite verbalization and questions. Encourage the child to explain his fear in detail, including when it started and what prompted it, and to ask questions related to it. Sometimes, children don't know what caused a fear, but they can usually explain what they are afraid of. For example, Carol, in Grade 4, was terrified to walk alone a single block home from school, yet she had always done this in the past. She had trouble explaining her fear until the teacher helped pin it down with leading questions. Their conversation went like this.

> *Teacher:* Didn't you walk home alone last year?
> *Carol:* Yes.
> *Teacher:* When did it start to feel scary?
> *Carol:* I dunno. Maybe a few weeks ago.
> *Teacher:* Did something bad happen on the way home?
> *Carol:* No.
> *Teacher:* Tell me what you think about when you think of walking home alone.
> *Carol:* Some guys coming to take me — you know — sex guys.

It turned out that Carol had seen a television news story of a young girl being abducted by a pedophile, and she had transferred the scene to her own neighborhood and to the walk home from school. The teacher invited Carol to ask questions about the issue, and Carol inquired about the possibility of it happening there, and what happened to the man and the girl who was abducted.

Self-disclose using "I" statements. Tell how you feel about the situation. Share your honest feelings: "I feel frightened by the thought of pedophiles in our community, too. It's not good to think you aren't safe . . ." By so doing, you are showing respect for the child's concern and giving credence to it.

Be honest. Being honest is very important, especially if the fear has reached the unreasoning stage. Answer questions truthfully. If there are no questions, try to provide enough honest information to allow the child better understanding of the issue at hand. Avoid too much information. Be concise and truthful. For example, the teacher above might have said, "I know that the abducted girl was returned home, and she got lots of help from her family and some other people, and that the man is in jail." If, however, Carol had asked about what the man had done to the girl, the teacher would truthfully say she didn't know and avoid that subject, the content of which denotes "too much information."

Another component of this step is to point out as tactfully as possible when a fear has reached unreasoning status. If the resulting behavior is non-productive — even, in some cases, ridiculous — try to get the child to recognize this. One way to achieve this is to pose a similar *fantasy* situation and invite discussion.

> *Example:* A boy called Danny stopped going to his soccer games even though he loved soccer because he was afraid someone might steal him away from the soccer field. Do you think that might have happened?

Allowing the child to see the risk situation from the point of view of another often helps to reduce the unreasoning nature of the fear.

Focus on the positive. Remind the child that most people are kind, caring, and helpful, and in Carol's case, that men like the one that prompted her fear are rare. Reinforce how the police force, parent watch groups, and teachers on playground duty all work hard to help keep her safe.

Create an action plan. Even though it will probably never be needed, developing an action plan with the student serves to reassure her and help her conquer the fear. In this case, Carol could walk home with a buddy; carry a cell phone and call home as she was leaving and possibly again after a half-block; or walk home while the teacher-on-duty watched and waved at various intervals. An action plan would help Carol feel safer.

Group Fears

Children are vulnerable. They are easily distracted and are quick to follow a leader. In addition, many of them are overly dramatic and love to embellish ideas or concerns before an audience. It's easy to see why a reasonable fear can readily escalate if or when shared with peers.

Consider the following true story. A 10-year-old heard a portion of a newscast on the car radio when his father was driving him to school. He *thought* he heard something about terrorists having weapons of mass destruction and targeting schools. When he asked his father about it, the man was distracted and simply

Good Idea

Using game format ("Let's play a pretend game . . ."), invite students to think of the silliest ways possible to deal with a suggested fear. For example, to deal with the fear of failure on a test: (1) run away from school, (2) burn all the tests, or (3) break a leg so you'd be in hospital. This game helps students see how ridiculous some fear-related behaviors are.

Good Idea

If young children are fearful about walking home from school either together or alone, tell them about "The Gate Game," created by two Grade 2 girls. The girls simply ran together from one gate to the next, touching each gate and catching their breaths at the gates. If the house had a sidewalk and no gate, they created an imaginary gate at some point adjacent to the house — they walked only on streets that had houses. The game distracted them from feeling anxious and also kept them close to "safe houses." When the first girl reached her home, she would wait at her own "gate" and watch her friend continue the game until she, too, was home.

Luckily, these girls lived quite close to each other, but a similar idea could be used with other children by reminding them to keep close enough to homes to "touch gates."

told his son not to worry. The boy had a reasonable fear of terrorist activity, but he had previously understood that the threat was not a danger to him. Unsure of exactly what he had heard but filled with the bubbling imagination of youth, he quickly told his peers that terrorists were bombing schools and, of course, the situation escalated from there. Students panicked. Teachers had no idea what was happening. It was a bizarre mess until one teacher traced the source of the story and put an end to it. Group fear can quickly turn to mob hysteria and panic. If this situation occurs, even though the fear may be grounded in reality, it has become unreasoning, and the teacher needs to take immediate action — what I call "Stop-Speak."

In Stop-Speak, the teacher uses a firm voice and a hand held up in the universal Stop position, and demands that all talk cease immediately. Following the use of Stop-Speak, the Formula Five for helping children deal with fear should be used. In the case provided above, during steps 1 and 3, the teacher would be wise to clarify the false information received by the boy. Apparently, the news anchor had been discussing two different stories, and the boy had somehow melded them into one. As a rule, once a fear is shown to be invalid, children will quickly drop it and go on to other pursuits.

I am not suggesting that teachers allow children to think risk-based fears are "silly." Teachers should point out that the original basis for the fear could have been real. "If you really did overhear a bomb threat, it would be very frightening." The teacher's instincts will tell her when to encourage a student to dismiss a fear and when to deal with the fear in more detail. A foolish, unfounded fear might be fear of tsunami in Alberta. If the fear had greater basis in reality, however, the teacher could adopt the Formula Five strategy above, and if necessary, involve parents or counselors.

Even for older children and adolescents, picture books are a good choice when discussing an area of concern because of their direct and simple handling of a problem. When using a picture book with a large group, you might want to highlight a few of the illustrations by showing them on an overhead so that the whole group can see and enjoy the images.

Serendipity Books (see example at right) are useful for almost any content area of this book. Each beautifully illustrated and written picture book has a moral, written on the front cover. The books are truly becoming classics in children's literature. I will refer to specific titles throughout *Teaching in Troubled Times*.

The article, "Fear of Failure: A Childhood Epidemic," can be found at www.keepingkidshealthy.com/parenting.../fear_of_failure.

Good Reads

The Sky Goes on Forever: A Book About Death for Children by Molly MacGregor
Brave Little Monster by Ken Baker (illustrated by Geoffrey Hayes)
The Monster Who Ate Darkness by Joyce Dunbar
Oscar and the Moth by Geoff Warin
Can't You Sleep, Little Bear? by Martin Waddell (illustrated by Barbara Firth)
Buttermilk by Stephen Cosgrove (illustrated by Robin James) (Serendipity Books)

Fear of Failure

Fear of failure, as an April 2005 article about an online study confirms, is almost an epidemic among children today. Although we all recognize that failure is a part of life, a way to learn and improve upon mistakes, when it becomes a fear, an *unreasoning* fear, it becomes a problem. This unreasoning fear of failure is directly related to risk taking and to the seemingly ever-increasing pressure that society tends to put on children to learn more, do more, be better while exposing them to the troubles of a chaotic world — too many children succumb and simply stop trying.

Consider the many areas in school where children might experience fear of failure: presenting a report, performing in a recital, playing a sport, writing a test, getting chosen for a team, to name a few. This fear of failure can cause them to pull back, to lessen the risk by "not doing the best possible," to therefore never achieve real success. Or, at the opposite extreme, it may cause excessive studying, sometimes long into the night where precious sleep is compromised and the child becomes more and more isolated from reality. Both of these reactions to the fear of failure present serious problems for teachers.

Failing is, of course, difficult, but more than that, it takes a punch at self-esteem; however, being afraid to try is even worse than failing. The if-I-don't-do-it-I-can't-fail attitude lies behind the apathetic and non-productive behaviors of far too many students. Many of them don't even recognize this as the reason for their lack of performance; they often consider themselves to be "lazy," "bored," or "too good" to do such mundane work. All of these potential reasons, coupled with lack of performance, lead to lowered self-esteem. What these students don't see is that their lack of trying is, in itself, a huge failure. They need to be taught how not to fear "striking out." Indeed, they may learn to appreciate these words of Babe Ruth: "Never let the fear of striking out make you afraid to swing."

The Formula Five below suggests a possible teacher intervention for dealing with fear of failure by avoidance. It works best in a one-on-one situation as every student's own fear of failure is different from that of his peers. The first step — redefining failure — serves as an excellent lesson for the entire class.

Redefine failure.
Identify the specific fear as a risk.
Determine fruitless responses.
Create an action plan.
Evaluate the action plan.

Formula Five: Dealing with Fear of Failure by Task Evasion

Redefine failure. Somehow, failure has become an almost *illegal* act. Many young people view failure as being "punishable," as something that breaks some unspoken, but well-known law of existence. At an orientation assembly one boy in Grade 7 asked, "What are the laws about failing in this school?" We all assumed he had simply misused the word "laws" and was referring to something less official, such as "standards" or "expectations," but in retrospect, I wonder . . . Most certainly, children view failure with anxiety and try to avoid it at all costs. The media tend to describe failure as negative, bad, or wrong. A person who is a failure is depicted as unpopular, unattractive, disliked — basically, a loser. It's easy to see how this definition of failure, connected as it is to loss of acceptance, love, and personal self-worth, is harmful to children. Failure is seen as a serious risk, a threat to one's happiness.

A teacher's job is to redefine failure in a positive manner. The following points will help.

- Failure is a chance to learn, to improve, to do better, to *be* better.
- It provides a situation where growth is possible.
- Failure reflects not taking responsibility for self; therefore, it opens doors for someone to become more responsible.
- Fear of failure often results from being too concerned with our culture's incorrect definition of success — a focus on popularity and appearance at the expense of what's best for self and others. This can lead to selfish, uncaring behavior, which is not what the student wants to show.
- Every failure offers a lesson within it. If identified, it will put someone well on the way to being successful next time.
- The only real way to fail is to avoid trying.

Identify the specific fear as a risk. In discussion, encourage the child to identify the specific fear of failure. Is it a fear of failing a test? of not hitting the ball in the softball game? of being the last one picked for a team in Phys. Ed.? Once the child can clearly state the fear, then point out that it prevents him from taking a risk: of writing the test, of playing the game, of being chosen last. By pointing out where he takes risks in other areas (e.g., presenting his report all alone, taking part in a spelling bee), you will help him to see the fear in a different manner. Remind him that risk taking is living — every moment of every day we take risks. Then, invite him to figure out exactly what the risk is. In most cases, the risk consists of being embarrassed or of upsetting someone else. Once he can identify the fear and then the risk, he is ready for the next step.

Determine fruitless responses. Children are masters at pretence. They avoid failure in several ways. For instance, they avoid doing the task: they pretend illness, loss of materials, or lack of motivation, or simply refuse. Or they may rationalize a failure with myriad excuses. "I would have done better but . . ." This not-my-fault scenario is common in schools. Often, the blame for lack of success is placed on the teacher. "She isn't fair . . ." A final way children avoid failure is more covert. They will work just enough to "get by" — that is, they avoid failure — but will not push themselves to be "better" in case they fail at this higher level of success. "I *could* get an honors mark, but I don't want to." This final method is an enormous frustration to the teacher who knows a child can do so much better, yet can't seem to encourage him or her to do so.

At this stage the teacher must help the child to realize exactly what she has been doing to avoid the possible failure. If the child cannot recognize it on her own or after leading questions such as "What do you do instead of . . . ," the teacher should tell the child what she thinks she does and ask if she would agree. Sometimes, just identifying the fruitless responses to a fear of failure is enough to initiate more positive behavior in the future.

Create an action plan. Identifying the fruitless responses and moving forward in small steps help the student find a way to better deal with this type of situation the next time it occurs. One possible action plan, given from a student's point of view, follows:

1. Next time, use Stop-Speak (in my mind) (page 15) and figure out what I'm afraid of and why.
2. I will allow myself two minutes to think about this carefully and ask myself who I'm helping and who I'm hurting.
3. Instead of [fill in with usual action], I will try a small step, such as [writing the test and expecting to pass — I'll improve my mark].
4. I'll ask myself what I learned, even if I do fail.

Evaluate the action plan. Return to the child in a few days or immediately after another situation in which you suspect he will fear failure, and do a follow-up. Ask how the plan worked, and if it needs changing in any way. Remember to revisit the redefinition of failure and reinforce even tiny steps in the right direction. If the action plan is shown not to be working, it is likely that the student is still resisting and not putting out effort. In that case, there are two alternatives to try: (1) using humor and (2) using bargaining.

- *Using Humor:* When you notice the student "inert," squat down to eye level and whisper, "What are you doing?" Don't use a sarcastic tone. Act curious. Probably, the answer will be "nothing" or a shrug. If you get "nothing," then say, with a twinkle in your voice so that the student knows you are teasing, "Well, you're doing an excellent job of it." If you get a shrug, say, "I think that means you're doing nothing and you're sure doing an excellent job of it." Keep the same light tone. I have never seen a student not at least smile when this happens, but whether she does or not, add, "I'd love to see the energy you're using to do nothing so well, put into a little . . ." Smile, and leave the desk side. This may be enough to stimulate at least a start. If not, then proceed to "Using Bargaining."

- *Using Bargaining:* This is a make-a-deal situation. Tell the student you just can't accept her doing nothing, no matter how good she is at it — keep the tone light — and say you want to make a deal with her. Ask her how much she *will* do, for example, the first two questions on a test or the first sentence of an essay. If she says "nothing," tell her that's not acceptable to you, and make a few suggestions, very *small* suggestions. Say: "I'm just not comfortable with you doing nothing. I feel like I'm not doing my job. How about you just do the first question? I'll settle for that this time." If you use "I" statements ("I feel . . .") and make the bargain easy enough, no student will reject it. After all, the student is getting permission to do only a tiny part of the task. One deal I made with a troubled Grade 4 student consisted of her writing only her name and just her first name at that. Of course, the next time the situation arises, which it will, increase your demands; the bargaining continues gradually until you are getting at least a reasonable effort.

For the child who *does* the task but does it poorly, the bargaining method works well. Say something like, "I see you got 67 percent on this math quiz. I'm just not feeling good about that because I know you can do better. When you get a mark in the 60s, I think I must not be doing a good job. Let's make a deal. How much higher do you think you can make your next mark?"

When dealing with a child who is exhibiting fear of failure, the important things to remember are to talk one-on-one, remain calm, avoid judging or criticizing, use "I" statements, use humor and bargaining when necessary, and keep returning to the child to check and recheck and recheck.

Overdoing as a way to avoid failure

Just as the child who avoids a task so as not to risk failing, the child who pushes himself to extremes for the same reason faces other risks — burnout, illness, and depression as well as all the negatives associated with isolation.

Consider the following true anecdote. Mary, 13, was the single child of wealthy parents who were both professionals with extremely high standards for their daughter. Mary was an average student who worked hard, but her parents wanted her to be the best student. In an attempt to reach their expectations, she started setting her alarm for 5 a.m. so that she could study for two hours before breakfast. This measure helped, but not enough. She set her alarm earlier and earlier until, unbeknownst to her parents, Mary was getting up at 2 a.m. every day, including weekends, to improve her marks. Her teacher noticed the in-class apathy, then the dark circles under her eyes, and questioned her privately. Mary declined to provide any information. The following day Mary passed out in the gym and was rushed to hospital where she was diagnosed with severe sleep deprivation. Mary's parents, aware only that their daughter was "pulling up her grades," were astonished when they found out how their daughter had tried to please them.

Teachers can help students avoid such overreactions to the fear of failure by employing the following tactics in class:

- valuing all accomplishments, not just the "top" ones
- discussing the importance of health-related measures, such as eight hours of sleep per night
- discussing the importance of social connectedness

- being alert to any physical changes in students and to any unusual changes in marks (Mary's marks were suddenly higher than would be expected from what the teacher already knew about her.)

In addition, teachers can be honest with parents as to the presumed abilities of their students. Telling parents their child is "brilliant" when he or she is not, or is able to achieve top marks when he or she isn't, is not only dishonest, but potentially harmful to the child. Perhaps teachers would not exaggerate that much, but the reality is that many professionals "mask" the truth and often provide misleading information to parents, perhaps with the intention of maintaining positive parent–child relationships or even of reducing how many angry or distraught parents they must deal with.

Parents want and deserve the truth. If Mary is functioning to the best of her ability, even though that doesn't necessarily mean at the top of the class, parents need that information. If parents have set unrealistic goals for Mary, it is the teacher's professional responsibility to honestly explain, using specific examples of Mary's work, why these aspirations may be out of reach.

As a final word about fear of failure, remember that failure in today's culture has a stigma attached to it, and children are hugely affected by cultural norms. Peer pressure is often far more important than the words of a teacher or even a parent, so the need to "not fail" may be greater than your encouraged "need to try." I would encourage teachers to keep trying; if the child doesn't seem to be learning how to deal with fear of failure, at least the messages will be recalled and, who knows, some day put to use. As civil rights leader Frederick Douglass wrote, "It's easier to build strong children than to mend broken men."

Head/Heart Reactions to Fear

There are many names for the "Head/Heart" idea, essentially the idea that we react to fearful situations either with our heads (thinking, reasoning) or with our hearts (instinct, gut feelings). As a rule, children act first with their hearts. Consequently, they often behave in a manner that they might have considered foolish had they been able to engage their heads first. For example, while surfing the Web a young child happens upon a horrific sight of a child being beaten. The act of extreme violence immediately grips his *heart* and terrifies him as he unconsciously puts himself into the scene. His stomach seizes and his pulse races. He lives the terror, and it instantly becomes an unreasoning fear. *What if someone beat me like that? Is the child dying? What if I die?*

On the other hand, an adult coming upon a similar image is able to use his head and reason that it is just an image, albeit a terrible one. This head/heart confusion in children can be effectively dealt with by teaching them to use the Stop-Think strategy. As obvious as this seems to adults, it isn't as obvious to children who far too often allow their hearts, their inner gut feelings, to get out of control, thus creating an exaggerated and possibly misplaced fear. So, talk with children about mentally saying "Stop-Think" when faced with an upsetting image. Similar to Stop-Speak, they are to begin by consciously *stopping* the flow of thoughts or ideas; they are then to *think* of three things:

1. Is this real or make-believe? (Older children should ask, "Is this fact or fiction?")
2. Could this actually happen here in . . .?
3. How can I deal appropriately with this image?

Dealing with fears

Discussion, writing, drama, and research all afford opportunities for students to explore and address their fears.

- *Whole-Class Discussions:* The following suggestions for leading a class discussion may help you to help students formulate answers to the three questions identified above.

  Is this real or make-believe, fact or fiction?
  Is it a cartoon or photograph?
  What is it trying to say?
  Why is the artist/photographer using fear?
  Can you turn your feelings (e.g., anger, upset, pain) towards the artist/ photographer instead of the character(s) being depicted? (That would be a more reasonable solution than experiencing feelings about the characters in the image.)

  Could this actually happen here in . . . ?
  Where do you (we) live? Where does the image suggest it is?
  How are the two locations different?
  What time of day/year is it in the image? Why do you think that is the case?
  Why could this *not* likely happen here?
  What are some positives about where we live that would make this image less likely to be here?

  How can I deal appropriately with this image?
  Categorize your feelings about it; then, bring them to your teacher (parent/ significant adult).
  Avoid keeping feelings inside. Discuss them with someone you trust.
  Avoid returning to the image. Delete it if on computer and avoid returning to the site. (Sometimes, children are drawn back to disturbing images much the same way adults are to the scene of an accident. Encourage them not to do this as it will refresh the associated fears.)

- *Individual Writing:* Write about the experience in a journal, write a fictional account of what "might" have happened as a result of the growing fear, or write a friendly letter advising a peer about the pitfalls of group fear.
- *Small-Group Drama Presentations:* Develop presentations related to the episode, making use of exaggerated reactions or ridiculous outcomes. For example, a group might act out the unreasoning fear of "going outside" (agoraphobia); two actors could tempt a third to leave the house by teasing him with small bites of a favorite food, until finally the fearful one falls down the steps, lands in a prickly bush, and says, "See! This is why I don't come outside." This comedic approach lessens the extreme fear associated with the initial reaction and enables the teacher to follow up with a calm, more realistic discussion which, in this case, would provide accurate information about the real condition.
- *Small-Group Discussions:* Talk about appropriate action plans related to the unreasoning fear; explore ways to prevent the fear from reoccurring.
- *Research:* Partners research the original base for the unreasoning fear and attempt to arrive at more realistic information that can be presented to the class.

- *Open-Ended Sentences:* Partners or small groups complete open-ended sentences related to the experience. Share as a class and compare responses. Possible sentence prompts:

  Fear is . . .

  One thing that makes a fear grow is . . .

  One thing that can be done when someone shares a fear that seems strange or wrong is . . .

  An example of a really tall-tale fear is . . .

  A good way to deal with a ridiculous fear is . . .

Hearts & Heads game

All fear is a reaction to a situation where risk or perception of risk is involved. As teachers you already understand how children view risk differently from adults. Children are concerned about their own safety and the safety of loved ones; they also fear separation from loved ones. All of their fears are based on these realities; all of their fears must be addressed with this in mind.

To help students better understand how "risk" or perception of risk defines us or makes us afraid on many levels, do the following activity. If presented as a game, children will respond more favorably.

Divide children into four or five separate groups, depending on how much control you desire over the game. (The whole class as four groups provides maximum control.) Randomly assign one of the following to each group: (1) Hearts, (2) Heads, (3) Judges, and (4) Lawyers. The teacher poses a frightening situation (see suggestions below), records it on the board, and allows about five minutes of discussion in the groups. During this time the Judges decide on a determining criterion which will be used to judge the presentations. This criterion is kept secret (see criteria suggestions below). The teacher can assist this group with suggestions, if necessary. Then, each group in sequence must present as follows:

1. *Lawyers:* They define the fear *as a risk* to the child, using terms that are as objective as possible.
2. *Hearts:* They describe how they would react "from their gut instincts" to the risk. They can act it out, list several reactions . . . whatever they feel their hearts would tell them to do.
3. *Heads:* They follow the same format as Hearts, but with the Heads point of view.
4. *Judges:* They are allowed about 60 seconds of quiet deliberation among themselves following the presentations; they must then make a decision and award the case in favor of either Hearts or Heads, depending on which group they felt made a presentation that most fit their predetermined requirements. Criteria that judges could adopt include reactions that are outrageous, funny, silly or inappropriate, sneaky or quiet, loud or raucous, likely to draw attention or a crowd, and unlikely (likely) to be successful.

Follow-up: Debriefing Hearts & Heads is important. The teacher can check for understanding about how the fear was based on a personal risk and about plausible ways to handle the initial risk. Students can journal what they learned, how they felt, what they might do if they experienced that risk situation. Children need to understand risk as a component of fear if they are to better handle the daily fears they will face.

Avoid suggesting "big" troubles, such as fear of war, disease, or terrorist activity; we don't want to put potential worries into vulnerable minds. Stick to "smaller" fears, such as those listed below, or ask children to identify the fears.

Possible Situations for Hearts & Heads

- Fear of spiders, ants, bees, crawling insects
- Fear of the dark in the closet or under the bed
- Fear of thunderstorms
- Fear of tests (e.g., math, science, social studies, language arts)

Hearts & Heads Game: Example

TEACHER: You come home from school. It's very cold, your parents are not home, and you have lost your key and your cell phone. Your neighbor's house is all dark.

LAWYERS: Through no fault of your own, you face the risk of being outside all night, cold, hungry, alone, afraid. You are terrified of being alone and of being in the dark. You are also afraid that someone might come along and abduct you.

HEARTS: We cry and curl up on the front step, start screaming so that someone who might hear us can offer help, run frantically to neighbors, and pound on the door even though we know they aren't home.

HEADS: We check to see if there's another key. When we can't find one, we try to climb in a window. If that doesn't work, we start walking — before it gets dark — to the nearest phone to call a relative or friend.

JUDGES: The case is awarded to the Hearts because our secret criterion was "loud," and they were screaming loudly.

Follow-up: Together, decide on the best way to handle being locked out. Discuss all possible difficulties, such as feeling cold, and come up with appropriate suggestions for dealing with them. Of course, the Judges' choice is seen as silly or funny, but the "best possible choice" must also be found.

As mentioned previously, children in today's troubled world can be fearful. Beyond all the usual demands placed on them, teachers today have yet another goal: to recognize and deal with their students' fears. I hope that this section will help them to find success in this area.

Good Reads

Who's Afraid of the Dark? by Leia A. Stinnett (Little Angel Books)
What's That Noise? by Michelle Edwards with Phyllis Root (illustrated by Paul Meisel)
Sheila Rae, the Brave by Kevin Henkes
Brave Irene by William Steig

Spontaneous Support

Teachers are well aware that they *should* do something to help their students deal with worries, fears, questions, and general anxieties related to today's troubled world and their precarious positions in it. That nefarious "should" can drive anyone crazy, especially when that anyone is an already overworked teacher. Part of the inherent tension in that *should* comes, I believe, from being unsure of what to do and how best to handle sensitive or hot topics. Of course, there is no pat answer, and certainly everyone, everywhere, seems to have an idea of how to proceed to the point where even the most dedicated researcher would have difficulty making a selection. Yet here I am offering another strategy, another plan. The difference is that this plan has been tried by teachers and proven to work. This Spontaneous Support strategy is quick and to-the-point. Best of all, it has already been fine-tuned for educators.

I appreciate that teachers do not always have the time to stop what they are doing and provide the *full* Spontaneous Support strategy. However, I encourage all adults who encounter a child's sensitive question to follow the steps as soon as possible afterwards. By asking a sensitive question or raising a source of unease, the child has made *you* the significant adult for this particular concern. Keep in mind, too, that if one student expresses a worry, many others will most likely have the same one and will benefit from Spontaneous Support. The good thing about Spontaneous Support is that it can be used for any trouble, worry, concern, or sensitive question that a child or group of children may pose.

Formula Five: Spontaneous Support Strategy

Look, listen, clarify.
Gather information.
Acknowledge and accept feelings.
Provide reassurance.
Lead a liberating activity.

Look, listen, clarify. Pay attention not only to what is being said, but also to non-verbal behaviors, such as hand wringing or lack of eye contact, that may hint at underlying anxiety; then, paraphrase the child's question to see if you have it right. Ask pertinent questions if in doubt. Child says, "I saw on TV that a little boy got his legs blown off and he was just going to school. What if that happened here too? Are the terrorists putting stuff here too?" Teacher paraphrases, "You saw a boy injured and are worried that that might happen to you." Teacher also clarifies by asking, "Did the little boy step on something?" Child answers, "A bomb."

Gather information. Quickly ask questions to determine what the child already knows or doesn't know. Doing this lets you know how much or how little information to provide. Teacher asks, "Do you know where this happened?" "What made you say 'terrorist'? Are you worried about terrorists here in ___?"

Acknowledge and accept feelings. Use positive words that convey your true thoughts. For example, say, "I understand." Avoid meaningless words such as, "It's all okay." Let the child know that his feelings are normal and that you, too, often feel that way. Provide permission to convey feelings by saying something like, "It makes me glad that you can tell me you are worried. I am worried [sad, concerned . . .] too because . . ."

Provide reassurance. Confirm, if true, or weaken if false the child's beliefs as simply as possible. "Yes, you are right. Many children have been killed." Or "I understand how you got the idea that . . . That would make me sad too. But I think the actual case is . . ." If talking with an entire class, summarize their beliefs and provide a simple sentence of truth: "Many of you are worried about injury to yourselves caused by terrorists. It's true that sometimes terrorists do harm to people even here in ___, but the chances of that happening are small, and we are doing everything we can to protect you." Keep the discussion short and to the point — dragging it out might increase fears and concerns. (*Teacher must be worried about this because we've been talking about it for ages.*)

Lead a liberating activity. That is, attempt to turn children's attention to something else, to an activity that will help them "move away" from the concern. This recommendation is not meant to downsize the initial concern, but to help children realize there are other ways to deal with it. For example, you might want to further the initial concern by inviting students, depending on ages, to write letters to or prepare shoeboxes of toiletries for children near or far who are in need or to research terrorist activity at some specific time in history (chosen by the teacher) with the goal being to gain historical awareness. These activities are "liberating" in that they move the students away from worrying about a situation and involve

These liberating activities, combined here for easy access by teachers, will be referred to throughout the book. They are numbered for ready reference in other sections of *Teaching in Troubled Times*.

them in taking some small action(s) that may help. We are all familiar with the I-can't-just-sit-here-and-do-nothing situation when we are worried about someone or something. We need to keep active at times like this, and kids are no different. Taking part in a liberating activity implies doing something, anything, other than worrying. The following list of "some-things" may be helpful.

Liberating activities

Invite students to do any of the following:

1. Explore your feelings by writing about the topic of concern in a journal.
2. Write a script to express feelings related to the topic, and with a few peers, act it out. (This activity is a small-group project but can also involve individual writing of possible "scripts.")
3. Depending on what you've learned about letter writing, write business or friendly letters. You might send queries to members of Parliament or other politicians, friendly letters to peacekeepers overseas, or letters of complaint to local media for airing upsetting footage of people in a disaster zone at a time when young children may be part of the audience.
4. Collect practical items (e.g., paper, pencils, toothbrushes) to make care packages for children in underdeveloped countries or for the poor in your community. It may be possible to support a campaign such as Operation Backpack by which Ontario's York Region Food Network gives out appropriately filled backpacks through the region's food banks.
5. Develop and carry out a plan to earn money to aid children living in poverty, either at home or abroad.
6. As a class, earn money to sponsor a child. It's important not to drop this sponsorship once it has been started, so plan for others to carry on when you leave off. Consider establishing a minimum sponsorship term, perhaps five years.
7. Create colorful posters drawing attention to the positives in your own environment (e.g., food, water, shelter).
8. Fantasize a perfect world and then write about it or illustrate it.
9. Arrange for someone in the community to talk to the class about an area of concern. Perhaps a military person could talk about our country's role in Afghanistan.
10. In groups, create lists of positive ideas for someone who has the power to change the world.
11. Collect new and used picture books, and arrange to send them to underdeveloped countries, Aboriginal communities, or local neighborhoods where poverty is recognized to be an issue. Look for vibrant pictures and simple text, especially if the books are to go to a community that speaks little English.
12. Create cartoon strips either using stick figures or filling in speech balloons that have been whitened out on favorite cartoons from a local newspaper. Cut out a cartoon, remove the text, and write your own "liberating" text. For example: "I'm so tired of eating dog food," a dog thinks. "I need someone to sponsor me and feed me properly."
13. Assume the identity of a favorite cartoon character (e.g., Charlie Brown) or super hero (e.g., Wolverine) and write a letter of complaint on an issue of concern from that point of view. You will likely find that you can write more freely and express feelings you might otherwise have difficulty expressing.

14. Write poetry about the troubling idea — doing so has an amazingly cathartic effect on most kids. The two forms I recommend are acrostics and free verse, both outlined below. Later, display the poetry in a hall so that other students can benefit from it. You might call the display "No Fear Here."

Poetry for Liberation

Acrostic (perfect for Grades 1–4)

- Start with the "worry word" written vertically.
- Add a phrase or a couple of describing words, the first word of which starts with the letter on that line.
- Encourage kids to use positive words only on the final line.

Worry Word: "Wars"

Acrostic

W orld fighting
A ll over the planet
R eally scary
S afe here at home in ____

Free Verse (perfect for older kids)

The uninhibited freedom of writing free verse appeals to children who can write thoughts in whatever form they want. Encourage them to use good descriptive words and phrases, and to end on a positive note. The example above was written by a 12-year-old girl.

Free Verse
Wars,
Every day I hear about fighting
Terrifying,
I wonder why
We have to kill each other
I want the world to love
Someday it will.

Musical Interlude

If the students need cheering up, be ready. Keep on hand a selection of music the students enjoy and, if possible, a CD player. A favorite recording artist is Raffi — you can use any of his selections. Although intended for young children, the selections can be enjoyed by people of any age, even adults, if presented with passion and humor. Raffi's "Brush Your Teeth" or a similar silly, repetitive melody will catch attention and bring smiles.

On the other hand: Cautions for teachers

Of course, as with any action a teacher takes, there are those pesky "avoids," the reminders of what *not* to do. Teachers are, happily, human, and like all members of the human race, are flawed. They make mistakes. Sometimes, having a list of things to avoid will help keep them on their toes.

I'll never forget the time a youngster who was known for her worrywart ways and constant whining came to me with yet another concern. I was in the middle of a difficult task on the computer (in honesty, *every* task on the computer was difficult for me) when she made her move.

"Teacher," she whined, "you know that kid who took a gun to school and killed all those kids and teachers?"

"Hmmmm," I replied, only half-listening.

"Well, what if there's a guy here who says he's gonna do that? What if he brings a gun to school and kills everyone too?"

"Oh, Jose," I said, never stopping my fingers tapping at the keys or looking at the girl who was leaning so close I could feel the heat, "that won't happen here. Don't be silly. This is Canada for heaven's sake."

I don't recall what she said after that and it wasn't until later that night I realized how cold and callous I had been. Jose was worried, *really* worried, about a real-life situation and I had downplayed her concern, foolish though I thought it to be; I had been so condescending that memory of my words made me gag. The trouble was real to her. She was right. I was wrong.

The warnings, or things to avoid, appear as a Formula Five. I have written them out as much for my sake as for the sake of others. I hope they will be helpful.

Don't ignore or downplay.
Don't use shallow or meaningless words.
Don't judge.
Don't argue.
Don't lecture.

Formula Five: What *Not* to Do When Exposed to a Child's Fears and Worries

Don't ignore or downplay. The child's concern is real to her; make it real to you too, regardless of what you are doing or feeling at the time. Try to recognize and feel the trouble through the child's eyes. Although children tend to exaggerate their fears and maybe to overreact, this doesn't mean the concerns should be treated lightly. Give the child and the child's concerns personal, sincere attention.

Don't use shallow or meaningless words. Avoid saying things like "don't be silly" or "don't worry — it will be fine." Telling someone *not* to worry might well be the best way to ensure further worrying. Say that you understand he or she is worried. "I can see you are worried about . . ." Note your own feelings about the situation and keep them real. "I'm worried, too." Or, "It doesn't worry me because . . ., but I do feel sad about it."

Don't judge. The child is worried; accept that. Similarly, avoid judging the relevancy or accuracy of the statement. If the child says there has been a shooting in the school and you know that to be an exaggeration, say something like, "I can understand why you'd believe that to be true. That would be very upsetting. However, the truth as I know it is . . ." Check the validity of the child's statement if you suspect there may be some truth behind it. It's better to be overcautious where children's fears are the issue; something may require attention.

Don't argue. It's not helpful to say, "I didn't hear anything about . . . You are probably mistaken. Now stop worrying over nothing." As well, avoid saying that the statement is wrong, or a lie or an exaggeration, even if you believe this to be so. Accept it at face value until you can deal with feelings and worries, and find out more information. You could be wrong. In either case, the child's worries are real.

Don't lecture. Instead of taking the professorial stance and providing the child with a lecture about the situation, use the Spontaneous Support, or discussion, method. Encourage expression of feelings, beliefs, and concerns.

The use of the Spontaneous Support strategy, together with cautions for teachers, will be referred to throughout the book as they represent important teaching interventions. The five major themes addressed here each contain many circumstances where teachers will find themselves in situations that call for their immediate use. I recommend that the strategy and cautions be committed to memory.

One word about parental involvement is needed here. When a student poses a troubling question or concern, a common response is to say, "Talk to your parent (or guardian)." Of course, parents should always be involved in their children's worries, but consider the following. If the child has brought the problem to a teacher not only does it require an immediate reaction, but it is possible he or she is unable to take it to a parent, perhaps because of parental absence, illness, exhaustion, to name a few. Remember, also, that by presenting the worry, the child is putting the teacher in a position of trust and authority, which must not be taken lightly. My best suggestion is to use the Spontaneous Support strategy or parts of it, and then suggest parental involvement after the initial anxiety has lessened. The point is, avoid shifting responsibility — deal with the issue in the best way possible.

CHAPTER 2

Concerning the World

"The world is not dangerous because of those who do harm but because of those who look at it without doing anything."
— Albert Einstein

The world has been given first billing among the book's five trouble themes because the terrible "state of affairs" of our planet earth came up again and again when I was talking to teachers. Most would agree that our planet is more perilous today than ever before, even than during the Cold War. There are wars or conflagrations in India, Pakistan, Korea, Iraq, Iran, Ethiopia, and Yemen, to name a few. All around the world many *lesser* battles are ongoing. In addition, in Third World countries, famine, disease, and illiteracy are the norm. In our own part of the globe, natural disasters are occurring with disturbing frequency. And in our own communities, news of diseases, such as H1N1, competes with stories of job losses and escalating numbers of people requiring — and sometimes not receiving — social assistance and food-bank bundles. The world is troubled, and kids know it.

Young people, no matter what their ages or how skillful their parents have been at isolating and protecting them, do not live in bubbles. They see and hear about the violent realities from peers, from newspapers, from magazines and, of course, from television and computers. Many of them carry gadgets that provide real-time information about real-life fears. They know they live in a world besieged by war. They are aware that we, the adults, have made a mess of the planet. They are aware that if they survive (and believe it or not, many worry that they won't) they will have to face a madness they did not create. They are also aware that the thoughts that plague them — these terrifying, anxiety-provoking thoughts, these overwhelming thoughts — are far too big and scary for little people like them.

Unfortunately, the knowledge that the fears are big-people concerns does not negate the "bad" thoughts. They remain. I will never forget the 10-year-old who told me he had read a billboard that said, "The future is friendly." He wondered who had put it up because — and I quote: "The future is scary, not friendly. I just saw on the news about more soldiers getting sent to Afghanistan. Jeff's dad's a soldier. He'll probably get killed. Lots of them do, you know. I think the future is pretty *un*friendly." I had no quick response. I wondered what other teachers might have said. I didn't know. But I did know, *do* know, that good teachers can and must help.

With that in mind, there are two areas of particular concern: telling the truth and dealing with activities that can specifically trigger children's worries. These particular fear-triggering activities include unlimited surfing of the World Wide Web, witnessing violence of any kind, witnessing depressing or cruel world situations, and easy accessibility to drugs, alcohol, or weapons.

Telling the Truth About World Problems

A point worth mentioning here pertains to the controversy of "to tell the truth or not to tell the truth." If the child has trusted the teacher with a worry, then he trusts the teacher for a truthful reply. There is an enormous debate about age-appropriate responses and at what age it is appropriate to be honest with children. The child has asked a tough question for which there are no easy answers. But a tough question cannot be deleted, watered down, or ignored. It is my firm belief that no matter what the child's age, the truth is the best possible answer.

Of course, some ways to handle the truth are better or less anxiety-inducing than others. For instance, if the question is about children dying of famine in South Africa ("Will more kids die?") or about being killed in Iraq ("Will soldiers kill kids?"), attempting to lessen the severity of the situation in an attempt to protect the child by denying the reality will not help. In most cases, the child knows the answer already, and a falsehood, even a "little white lie," could cause even further concern. *Why won't teacher tell me the truth? Is it that bad? Am I going to die too?* Honest talk is needed. An honest answer without gory or embellished details is best. For example, the teacher might agree that that war (disease, famine) is terrible and then say we have little control over it, and yes, some children might die. This answer will reassure the child that the teacher is seriously considering what he said and is giving an honest answer. The teacher then follows this up with reassurances about the immediate safety of the child or children. Because the initial answer has been honest and straightforward, the child will believe the reassurances and feel less worried. However, if the teacher had lied initially by offering pat phrases or platitudes (e.g., "We have nothing to worry about because we are good people"), the child will recognize a falsehood immediately and put no faith in the reassurances.

By *reassuring* I mean to state concisely and simply that everything is being done to protect the child. "Some children might die, but this is happening far away and there is no chance of soldiers coming here or killing children here because we have troops to protect us, and the war is not here in . . ." When possible, say exactly what this "protection" is and attempt to defuse worries that are inappropriate or exaggerated. Again, it is important to tell the truth. Lying is actually easier for the adult. ("No, of course, no kids will be hurt — soldiers don't kill kids.") But it can create more fears and questions. Be honest. Be empathetic. Be supportive. Follow, as soon as possible, the steps in Spontaneous Support (see pages 23–24).

"Today" Activities That Can Trigger Children's World Worries

So, what are these worry-triggering activities and situations?

We know that concerned and compassionate adults make every attempt to protect children from pursuits that may trigger concerns, worries, or fears, but in reality, total protection is impossible. As I mentioned previously, children do not live in bubbles; they live in an often nasty and frightening world, and are exposed to its unpleasantness regardless of what adults do or do not do. Certain activities and situations, however, seem to be more conducive to fear and worry than others.

If we can first identify the activities or typical situations that can have profoundly negative effects on children, we can take the next step, which is to remove or at least reduce their involvement with those pursuits. We have no control over world catastrophes, acts of terrorism, natural disasters, rampant poverty and disease, the easy accessibility of drugs and alcohol, or the failing economy. These conditions exist. Kids know all about them. What we *do* have control over are activities in which our students take part and that tie directly into these world troubles. I refer to these sources of distress as "fear-triggering activities or situations." They are activities that result in, literally, too much information or too readily available product.

As a good example of too much information, a child surfing the Web in an uncontrolled manner could happen upon sites portraying violence, disasters, wars, and so on. The fear-triggering activity, in this case, is the Web surfing without controls. In a perfect world, there would be no need for those controls. This is not a perfect world.

Another fear-triggering situation, one related to too readily available product, would be the appearance of drug-peddlers outside elementary schools. In a perfect world, they would never think of approaching young children with their drugs. Again, this is not a perfect world.

Of course, the Internet is not the only source of negatively charged information readily accessible to young people. They are surrounded by visuals, auditory cues, movies, television programs, video games, and peers who think they know everything. Certain activities, however, lend themselves more readily than others to children's exposure to disturbing material, and over these fear-triggering activities adults can exert some control. These fear-triggering activities or situations are identified in the box below — all adults should be familiar with them. Keep in mind I am dealing only with activities exposing frightening or harmful *world* issues at this point and situations more common today than in the past. There are probably many other instances that negatively affect our students, but teachers mentioned those below most frequently.

Each of these activities is more troublesome today than in the past, I believe, due to the current state of our world as well as the advanced state of technology we *enjoy*. In other words, the fact that these activities exist is a symptom of today's troubled world; they would not have posed the same level of concern when we, for example, attended school because there were fewer *troubles* and information about them was not as easily obtained.

One word of caution: If teachers are to assist children in moving towards independence, then they cannot, *must* not choose to ignore a negative situation when it arises. Children want, and deserve, honesty. They don't want to be given condescending responses, pat phrases, or Pollyanna reports — they want the truth. The cruel facts of life today are a reality. We do our students no good by pretending that negative situations do not exist. As teachers, we must be prepared to deal with topics no matter how painful, sensitive, or depressing they may be, honestly and openly. The trick is in knowing *how* to (see Formula Five: Spontaneous Support Strategy on pages 23–24).

Unlimited Surfing of the World Wide Web

I refer to unlimited surfing as a "world" trouble because technology has exceeded all expectations and opened all doors to everything the world has to offer. Unfortunately, that includes the not-so-nice with the nice. Children today are not even tied to personal computers, laptops, or notebooks; they can access horrific information about a world in chaos on their phones. Many of them can Google, blog,

Good Idea

When a child asks a sensitive question or poses a world worry trouble, avoid ignoring or deflecting it. Reassure the child about personal safety immediately and then return to the issue later.

Tweet, and, of course, phone 24 hours a day. This means they can conceivably be exposed to unsavory situations 24 hours a day, too.

All adults want to control what their children see and hear, but not all adults know how to do this effectively. There are myriad sites offering advice to parents and teachers for monitoring children's Internet access, so many that it becomes almost impossible to decide which ideas to use and which to delete. In fact, the time required to search all the sites for nuggets of information is never-ending, and what teacher (or parent) is blessed with never-ending time? Consequently, when allowing students to use the Internet, I suggest the following format.

Initial talk time

Discussions with children are always the first step. The following Formula Five suggests a comprehensive talk-to-kids pre-surfing plan. It appears to be a time-consuming activity, but it is not. All five parts of the Formula Five can be carried out in fewer than 10 minutes. In any event, keep the pre-computer talk quick and to-the-point — kids are eager to get started and probably not so eager to have a discussion. Without these 10 minutes, though, damage control necessary for unhappy outcomes can take so much longer.

Explain concerns.
Discuss purpose and curriculum connections.
Set expectations.
Discuss consequences.
Recheck.

Formula Five: Pre-computer Talk

Explain concerns. Lead a discussion about computer and Internet use, and avoid pussyfooting around the topics of concern. Specifically, explain your concerns, explain what kids must do and not do as a result of these concerns, and open the floor for discussion.

Possible concerns:

- Adult-based sites with disturbing content
- Chat rooms that can invade privacy and cause even more serious problems, such as unsavory individuals knowing too much about the child. For instance if a child provides personal information or identification to someone met in a chat room, the child may be putting him/herself at risk for cyber-bullying or other forms of even more serious abuse.
- Sites showing unnecessary violence, which has been *proven* to be detrimental to young eyes
- Sites that display content that children would not understand and could misinterpret

"Yes, But" Motivator

For some pre-computer use, you may wish to involve the students in a quick game that will remind them of the pros and cons of computer use, as well as getting the attention of any daydreamers. The game is played as a class or in pairs for about 60 seconds. Example:
A: Computers are useful.
B: Yes, but they can freeze.
A: Yes, but the Internet is filled with information.
B: Yes, but there are bad sites too.
A: Yes, but you don't have to download them.

Discuss purpose and curriculum connections. Whether or not you begin with a motivator such as "Yes, But," an initial talk time is mandatory. It should first and foremost review exactly what the students are searching for. In other words, what is the purpose of the search? Random searching usually leads to inappropriate site visiting. Every safe search begins with a reason to search as opposed to random surfing. Kids get into trouble only when they are unfocused, when they allow their natural curiosities to lead the way. If they have a purpose, a specific reason for searching, together with a concise set of well-understood expectations and consequences, there will be less trouble. The reason, of course, should be tied directly to curriculum objectives (e.g., researching a social studies topic about history). Once the reason has been defined, the teacher prepares the curriculum path, which begins with identifying specific areas to be searched based on the general topic.

1. List relevant areas as a group on the board or as individuals in notebooks.
2. Pull out possible safe search words from the selected areas. If done as a whole class, the teacher has obvious control; if individuals assume this role, some sort of adult check is needed before proceeding to the next step.
3. Discuss selection of safe search words to determine if they fit the criteria (see "Teaching safe searching," page 32).
4. When searching, cross out search words as they are used.

Set expectations. During initial discussions, expectations regarding appropriate computer and Internet use must be clear. Even if you have told the students many times before, quickly review these again. If you feel that the students know the expectations, ask them to review them orally for you. Of course, the expectations must be realistic, consistent, and easily monitored. In the classroom setting, the teacher can list expectations on the board or a wall chart and refer to them before every online period.

Sample expectations:

- View only sites that we feel are useful and safe, and that we have listed or agreed upon in class.
- If you find a new site, get it okayed before using it.
- Use the computer wisely and with discretion. That means no marking of the computer or drinks, gum, or edibles.
- The computer is a tool for mature use — make sure you use it in that manner.

Discuss or review consequences. It is not enough to set expectations. They need to be complemented by realistic and manageable consequences. As a quick part of the pre-computer use discussion, review your consequences for misuse.

Possible consequences:

- You will lose use of the computer for one week.
- You will lose use of e-mail for . . .
- You will be required to write a 1,000-word paper on the misuse of the Internet and the problems this can cause for young people.

Recheck. Provide a quick reminder of how you will be checking to see how students are doing and following your expectations. Be positive. We all know that students are outstanding examples of the self-fulfilling prophecy. If the teacher implies through word or nonverbal communication that she suspects even a hint of foul play, she will surely get it. Simply remind students of their good fortune in having access to so much information and of their responsibilities related to that. Send the students off with your confidence and respect. In other words, tell them that you know they will search wisely and appropriately: "I know you will all search wisely and find many excellent sites."

Remind them that following their time at the computers, you will have another quick discussion, a post-search check, in which they will share information about sites. You might ask:

- "How many sites did you visit?"
- "Which sites were the most useful? the least useful?"
- "Did you accidentally log on to a site you didn't intend to visit? What did you do?"

As a final note to this Formula Five, emphasize the importance of talking to students about what you expect, why you expect it, and what will happen should

Good Idea

Share the expectations you have set for online use with students' parents. Doing this allows them to adopt the same or similar ones, and reassures them as to in-class use of the Internet.

Good Idea

As another check, prompt students to keep records of sites visited. They can present or hand in the records with their assignments.

they disregard these expectations. See the wonderful Web page www.komando.com/kids/commandments.aspx. It features "The Kim Komando 10 Commandments for Kids Online." In addition to pre-computer talk, I recommend using these commandments or creating similar ones and having students sign them, in the form of a contract between you and them. Doing this makes setting expectations more authentic and gives it credence.

Open talk time

This is a period of time set aside, say, twice weekly or maybe 10 minutes daily depending on your schedule, when you are available for one-on-one talk with students about concerns they may have with or resulting from online work. Explain that this open talk time is specifically for them to share anything that is bothering them about online experiences. Perhaps a child is having technical problems (e.g., unable to access or download and is embarrassed to discuss them in front of techie-savvy peers). Or it may be that she happened upon a disturbing or frightening site.

Provide an example of a problem. "Perhaps, you accidentally got on to an adult site that had disturbing images or asked for your name, and even though you didn't provide it, you may feel worried . . ." Reassure students that what they say will be confidential unless, of course, you feel there is a real danger to them. In that case, explain that you will, with them, take whatever measures you feel are necessary. Nothing will be done "behind their backs."

Sometimes, students will come to open talk time, but find it difficult to talk. Perhaps they feel embarrassed or shy or simply can't find the right words. Be prepared to prompt with open-ended statements and then allow a few seconds of wait time for the student to respond before prompting again.

Sample prompts:

- "You opened a site that made you feel . . ."
- "By accident you found a site that was disturbing because . . ."
- "One of the sites you opened was about . . ."
- "You seem upset by something you discovered . . ."
- "The class rule for Internet use that you broke was . . ."

Close open talk time by summarizing what was discussed and reassuring the student that she did the best thing by telling you about it. Help her find better ways to search in the future.

Teaching safe searching

When it comes to safe searching, there are strategies for identifying the best words and phrases for the search.

We have all had the experience of typing in search words only to have a host of inappropriate sites pop up. Sometimes, these sites may be just too distracting to children and their natural curiosities prod them to look further. Our job is to help them choose the best search words so that this doesn't happen.

Kids have been quick to learn that all they have to do is type in whatever comes to mind and many pages are made available by the search engine. Adults must teach them to first think carefully about what they are searching and select the best keywords *before* pushing Enter. I know that all teachers today have dealt with this problem, but sometimes it helps to have a quick review or reinforcement.

Search facts to share:
- Every word counts.
- Searchers can use either lower or upper case letters.
- Most of the time, punctuation can be ignored. It's unnecessary when typing keywords into the browser. It must be used correctly, however, in e-mail or Web addresses.
- Simple is best.

It is worthwhile to point out that once keywords have been chosen, they can be entered into the browser in any order with the same results. In other words, "Indian elephant size" will provide the same results as "elephant size Indian." Random selection, that is, no specific order, works when searching, as long as the chosen words are specific.

Tips on simplifying choice of search words:
- Enter names first (e.g., Nike shoes), then location (e.g., Nike shoes Toronto). Students do well with this approach. Although this sequence is not strictly necessary, it provides a consistent construct for them.
- Think like a machine. Instead of "What do I do if I feel like vomiting," write "nausea."
- Use as few words as possible while making every word count — every word limits the search: "dogs sale Edmonton" will be more effective than "I want to buy a puppy in Edmonton."
- Avoid multiple meaning words. For example, when referring to a drama script, choose "script" rather than "play."
- Use specific words. For example, instead of "activity," choose "gymnastics."
- When in doubt, ask for help, or use a dictionary or thesaurus to find a better word.

Fast Four Motivator

Here is an activity for expanding on the idea of using the best search words.

1. Partners choose four words they would use to search a teacher-defined topic, for example, Which are bigger — Indian elephants or African elephants? To heighten Fast Four as a game, the teacher can provide a short time frame, such as 60 seconds, to determine the four best words, which students write down. No changes are allowed once time is up.
2. The teacher randomly draws words from her word bin, either pulling words on small scraps of paper or reading from a list of appropriate words. For the topic above, obvious words include elephant, size, variety, Africa, and India. Words are crossed off if the teacher calls them. Most pairs will have the same or similar search words and will, therefore, be "winners." It is quite possible all pairs will be winners, but if some pairs have different words, they are allowed to "justify," or explain, their choice of words. If they can justify to the teacher's satisfaction, they are also winners.

Further to this idea of choosing the best keywords, it is worthwhile to note that there are many safeguards to protect children from unlimited surfing. Most adults are familiar with them. The following are excellent.

- *Google:* At main page and without punctuation, type "safe search for kids." By doing so, you will open the "using safe search filter by Google," which will automatically filter the following searches.
- *MSN Search:* Use the Safe Search Filter on the Settings page.
- *Yahoo:* On the Search Preferences page (http://search.yahoo.com/preferences), select "Edit" next to SafeSearch; then select "Filter out adult Web, video, and image search results — SafeSearch On." Click "Save."

Good Reads

How to Find Almost Anything on the Internet: A Kid's Guide to Sage Searching by Ted Pedersen and Francis Moss
Cyber-Safe Kids, Cyber-Savvy Teens by Nancy E. Willard (for adults)

Children Witnessing Violence of Any Kind

I am including the witnessing of violence — domestic, community, or world-wide — as a "world" trouble because violence happens frequently, graphically, and appallingly, and teachers will want to offer whatever help they can to students to deal with the fears that accompany this, at least while they are within the school setting.

Choosing the best help

A plethora of information is available to educators for helping their students deal with violence. In fact, the sheer volume of information makes it almost inaccessible. Consequently, *Teaching in Troubled Times* distills the best help into concise, usable packages for ready teacher access. With this in mind, the term *violence* will not be broken up into its many aspects, including domestic violence, terrorism, homicide, and bullying. It will be considered an umbrella theme representing any kind of violent act that would distress children. I believe that no matter the degree of violence, if a child is upset, the teacher's stance should always be the same: to intervene quickly and effectively. A comment from Newton N. Minow gives support to that idea. "Children will watch anything, and when a broadcaster uses crime and violence and other shoddy devices to monopolize a child's attention, it's worse than taking candy from a baby," he writes. "It is taking precious time from the process of growing up." Exposure to violence is, however, a reality of our troubled world, a fact of life that, if we cannot change, we can at least accept and face with courage, and offer helpful support for our students.

For teachers some basic facts are important. Children in our classrooms who have seen or heard violence of any kind may not present any overt signs of disturbance. That they are silent bystanders to hostility and aggression does not mean they are accepting of it or unbothered by it. They may be experiencing fear, anxiety, anger, or a variety of other emotions. They may react by becoming unduly timid or by acting-out and becoming violent themselves. Most certainly, witnessing violence scars them in some way, and psychological scars frequently remain hidden.

So, what can we do?

First, it's important to appreciate that long before they turn up in our classrooms, most, if not all of our students have witnessed violence on television, on the Internet, in magazines, in movies, in the streets, on playgrounds, and perhaps even in their homes. Psychologists talk about ongoing violence as opposed to single-incident violence, about varying negative effects in children, from nightmares to post-traumatic distress disorder. There are suggestions that children's exposure to violence can either produce violent behavior or desensitize the children towards additional violence, thereby almost permitting or even glorifying violent acts. The more one reads, the more it becomes evident that the only consensus among psychologists as to the effects of violence on children is that it is "not good."

So, let's examine what we, as teachers, know. Children are exposed to violence — that's a given. We can prevent some of that exposure by controlling Internet use, reading selections, in-class films, and so on, but acts of violence are insidious; they pop up everywhere all the time. Given that our students do not live in a perfect, violence-free world, what can we do to help?

Consider the following. A Grade 5 student whom I'll call Kevin told his teacher he had seen an advertisement for an upcoming movie in which "big explosions blew up everything and pieces of people were flying everywhere — one man had no arms and no legs and he was still alive." This is a horrific image, one no young person should have to see, yet television stations often show trailers of Restricted or adult-only movies, and children sitting in front of the television are quick to watch. Of course, it would be great if every time a child watches television, browses the Internet, or skims a magazine in a store, all violent images were blocked; however, this is not the case and consequently, teachers get statements such as the one from Kevin.

Kevin's teacher shared with me that she was initially shocked and didn't know what to say, especially since her student had appeared excited, not disturbed. Before she had a chance to respond, one of the other students shouted, "Cool," and an animated discussion about violent explosions and flying body parts erupted. The teacher gathered her composure, demanded a stop to the discussion, and said that those sorts of images made her feel sad and scared. Then she asked her students, How did such images make them feel? Apparently, this question steered the discussion in a different direction, one about feelings and fears, one that she could better control, but she confessed that she had been totally shaken by the episode.

The point of this anecdote? Kids witness violence and do not all react to it in the same manner. Teachers must be prepared to counter appropriately. Using the Spontaneous Support strategy works well when discussing a violent act, with a bit more emphasis on encouraging emotional reactions and closure.

Although the steps below are similar to those of the Spontaneous Support strategy, teacher behaviors vary according to the severity of the act and the child's ability to describe it. The following Formula Five summarizes teacher interventions for violence.

Formula Five: Teacher "Violence" Intervention

Look and listen.
Clarify.
Accept without judgment.
Encourage reactions or emotions.
Encourage closure.

Look and listen. Give full attention to what is being said. Usually when a child is talking about a violent act that is bothering him, he will talk too quickly and ramble and have difficulty making himself clear. He may exaggerate and embellish what he has witnessed. Often, the more attentive his audience, especially peers, the more colorful his description. It is important to try to remove unnecessary or overly descriptive parts by interjecting a paraphrase that covers only the basics. If the child is talking about body parts, you might say, "People were killed." Encourage "slow talk"; put your hand on the child's shoulder or arm to calm him down and ask him to speak slowly and carefully. Maintain eye contact by getting to the child's level. By doing this, it becomes more difficult for the child to become hysterical or to deliver a rapidly worsening tale.

Clarify. Ask questions and restate what you think the child has said in an attempt to get to the truth of the problem. Try to separate the child's emotions from the actual incident. Formulate the concern into one succinct statement and ask if that is a correct description of the incident. If the child says "no," ask more questions and try again. It is important to get the details right so that you can accurately help her to move on, but equally important not to elaborate or embellish.

Accept without judgment. At this point avoid adding any judgmental statements, such as "That was a terrible thing." Just accept the description of the incident and accept the child's feelings. "You are obviously upset and frightened by . . ." It is helpful to add a statement of self-disclosure, such as "That would frighten me and make me feel upset."

Encourage reactions or emotions. Once you have clarified the incident, encourage additional emotions from the child, perhaps saying, "You are frightened. Are you angry too? What else do you feel when you think of . . .?" Invite possible desired reactions by asking questions such as these: "What does . . . make you feel like doing?" "What do you want to do right now?" If dealing with a whole class or group of children, invite all to take part in the discussion about feelings. Try to determine the general consensus and formulate a statement: "It seems we all feel . . ."

Encourage closure. If necessary, help the child to see how the reaction she would like to make is inappropriate: "You would like to shoot the bad guy, but that would make you a murderer." Help her to understand that the emotions she is feeling are normal and there are ways to handle them. For example, suggest she get involved in one of the Liberating activities (see pages 24–25) as a method of closure. If dealing with a group or class, involve them in a closure activity for small groups (3–4 students) or partners: see numbers 2, 12, 13, and 14.

Or Else Motivator

This activity will lead nicely into a discussion about violence. Its name comes from the common expression ". . . or else," which is usually offered as a rather threatening ultimatum, but in this case means the opposite. The "or else" will precede a positive alternative to a more violent reaction.

1. In small groups or pairs, students respond to a "situation" that the teacher describes aloud or puts on overhead. They are given a time limit to come up with the best "or else" alternative they can.
2. At the end of the time, answers are compared, and the entire group tries to choose the best "or else." Be sure to point out that this is not a competition, but an exercise in expanding their awareness.

Possible situations:

- Two kids are fighting in the alley and one is getting beaten up. You decide to help the underdog so get into the fight OR ELSE . . .
- Your brother is shouting at your mom because he wants a later curfew. You agree so you start shouting too OR ELSE . . .
- The other team in (soccer, basketball, hockey, . . .) is playing unfairly and roughing up your smallest players. Your captain takes a punch at one of their players. You decide to join in OR ELSE . . .
- A bully and his gang are throwing rocks at a dog. They invite you to join. You are afraid of the bully so you join in OR ELSE . . .

General suggestions for teachers dealing, in class, with world violence

Even when teachers use good strategies such as Formula Five: Teacher "Violence" Intervention, sometimes these aren't enough and they require more assistance. The following suggestions should be employed in any discussion about violence or the results of it, including fears, worries, and various covert or overt behaviors.

1. Before beginning a discussion, remind students that your class is a safe, caring place, and review any simple discussion rules you may have, such as these: don't interrupt, express feelings, ask questions, and listen to others.
2. Always acknowledge that the situation is frightening for you as well as for the children. Feelings of fear are worse when kept hidden.

3. Although you have admitted that the situation is frightening for you, too, avoid acting with alarm or outward fear.

4. Appreciate that the children are probably confused about what exactly has happened and will need explanations. Tell the truth, but keep the description simple.

5. Listen more than talk. You are not delivering a lecture. Answer any questions as truthfully as you feel confident in doing, and then listen some more. Don't answer any questions not asked, and don't make assumptions about what the kids know or what they want to know — ask them.

6. If students (or some students) seem reluctant to talk and your teacher's instinct tells you they would benefit from talking, ask leading questions: "Do you ever think about . . .? What feelings does the mind picture of . . . bring to you? Have you heard anyone, maybe your parents, talking about . . .?"

7. If some children avoid talking even after you have provided prompting questions, respect their right to silence and don't push. At a later time you can approach the child(ren) one-on-one and try again if you think it's necessary.

8. Be calm and reassure the students that those in power (e.g., teachers, parents, police, government) have everything under control. Demonstrate your own faith in these powers.

9. Encourage talk about emotions. How are they feeling? It's probable that there are a variety of different feelings, some powerful, others less so. Point out that all feelings are normal and that strong emotional reactions are healthy and acceptable.

10. Ensure that students don't exaggerate or embellish ideas when talking. Keep discussions on topic and remind children often that rumors and tall tales are not allowed in the talk. Stay in control of the discussion, guide it, encourage participation, but don't talk more than is absolutely necessary.

Good Idea

As soon as possible following a discussion about a disturbing topic, such as one based on a violent act, return the class to normal pursuits. Doing this reassures students that life goes on as before.

Teacher traps in dealing with world violence

Even the most conscientious teacher can fall into a teacher trap when leading a "tough" discussion. I recall the time I was talking with adolescents about school violence, based on the Columbine disaster, and suddenly realized the entire group was silently watching me with huge eyes. I had been disclosing far too much information, obviously more than they previously had or needed to know, and had terrified them. Reassuring the group and explaining that I got carried away did not make me or them feel a whole lot better. It would have been far better to have avoided the situation; hence, Formula Five: Avoiding Teacher Traps When Dealing with Violence.

Be brief.
Manage personal emotions.
Tell the truth.
Listen.
Assume the child's point of view.

Formula Five: Avoiding Teacher Traps When Dealing with Violence

Be brief. As mentioned in the previous paragraph, it's quite possible to get carried away and offer the students far too much information. We are, after all, teachers. Our job is to dispense information. But in the case of the tough-topic discussion, we must allow the students to talk. Our job is to mediate and provide simple answers, explanations, and clarifications only as necessary. If a child asks a question, answer only that question — don't elaborate or get sidetracked.

Manage personal emotions. Teachers are compassionate, usually highly emotional people, so it's quite easy to see how personal emotions can jump right into a discussion, coloring words and possibly affecting students' views and feelings. For instance, when talking with the students about the Columbine tragedy, it was difficult not to show extreme distaste for the killer, but to do so would have interfered with the objectivity of my words.

Tell the truth. This recommendation has come up previously, but it's so important — and so frequently a teacher trap — that it is mentioned again here. If a child asks a question, the teacher must provide a truthful answer. Naturally, the teacher will couch a response in words familiar to the child and will provide any reassurance necessary, but avoiding the truth because it is frightening is not the correct approach to take, especially during a tough-topic discussion.

Listen. Teachers talk; kids listen. That's the age-old way of teachers and students, and although we now understand that there are better approaches to learning, it's still sometimes difficult for teachers to remain silent and listen. Doing this is especially the case when kids are discussing a tough topic and are sharing powerful emotions. The conscientious teacher feels the need to jump in and add to the conversation, to talk, to lead, to reassure. Yet the importance of *just listening* as a reassurance tool cannot be overestimated. By listening, *really* listening, the teacher gives credence to the children's words and shows respect, thereby offering silent reassurance.

Assume the child's point of view. Sometimes, during those tough-topic discussions teachers fall into the teaching mode instead of forcing themselves to see the issues through a child's eyes. Kids see "bad" situations differently from adults, and a tough-topic discussion can be effectively directed only if the teacher remembers to adopt the child's point of view. For example, in regards to the Columbine murders, an adult (a teacher) might be considering the horror to the parents and community, while a child would probably focus on personal safety in his own school.

World Violence and Stereotyping

I recall vividly an instance of a young boy in Grade 4 telling his peer group about something he had overheard his father saying. Although I can't remember the exact words, the gist of them went something like this: "And my dad said anyone who wears a turban is likely working with those Taliban and so we should tell them they aren't welcome in our neighborhood. And I saw a dead cat in the alley. I think the turban guy probably killed it." Apparently, a new family had moved into a home in the boy's neighborhood and the family's presence was causing alarm simply because their dress and manners were somewhat different. I readily bring to mind now the sick feeling I had when I overheard the student. How was I to argue a position taken by his father, even though I knew it was wrong? At the time I noted how quick the boy was to attach violence, the dead cat, to the stereotype he already held of the man and his family and believed that there was nothing I could say or do to remedy the situation. Since that day I have come to think that teachers can, and must, work towards the eradication of stereotyping, with a careful focus on that about turbans (see page 41). The dilemma is, of course, how to accomplish this goal.

There are several reasons why stereotyping is worrisome in today's classroom. To begin with, our world is troubled, and violence appears to be erupting more frequently and more close to home (e.g., school shootings). Second, we are a multicultural society. Every classroom houses students of a variety of cultures, colors, ethnic groups, races, and, of course, abilities, making the "fodder for stereotyping" readily available. For example, if a child brings to school a parent's anger about another race and a child of that race is in the classroom, that child is likely to be the brunt of racial stereotyping. Third, the media, so readily accessible and available to all children, tend to promote stereotyping (e.g., the impoverished Latino mother loses in court, the black man gets beaten by police). When our vulnerable children are immersed in this culture of stereotyping, much of which is tied to or based on violent acts, this is, I believe, a modern "world trouble." Was this so great a problem in the classrooms 20 or 30 years ago? I think not. What can teachers do?

One good way is to make constructive use of the violence children see on television, in movies, in video games, and on eye-catching front-page newspaper photos is by talking with them about it and drawing attention to the foolish covert and overt acts of stereotyping. When children witness violence, they do two things: they blame someone, and they feel strong emotion directly related to the blamed person as well as for the victim(s). If, as teachers, we point out the errors in their accusations, which far too often are based on stereotyping or result in stereotyping, we can provide an important life lesson. Sometimes, by debunking the stereotypical myth, we also help to defuse some of the negative emotions associated with the violent acts. For example, consider the case of the boy and the dead cat. By discussing all the ways the cat could have died and most probably *did* die, we can remove blame from the new neighbor. Discussion about the beauty and importance of different cultures among us can help to alleviate negative feelings. What the teacher has done is used a violent act to teach a spontaneous lesson about stereotyping.

I think we can agree that media violence tends to keep alive myths about particular types, groups, races, or genders, and we can see how vulnerable children can get caught up in the beliefs. Many adults as well as children openly reject the idea that they stereotype certain people (e.g., blacks are stereotyped as being uneducated and violent), yet unconsciously they do it. Consider meeting two men on a dark street: a poorly dressed white and an equally poorly dressed black. From whom would most people shy away? In this sort of situation blacks have attested to noticing subtle signs of unease from Caucasians — and similarly, Caucasians have noted the same from blacks. A black might avoid looking at or move as far away as possible from the poorly dressed Caucasian, and vice versa. These signs are examples of unconscious stereotyping, which is often promoted by the media. Consider how often a down-and-out, poorly dressed person is depicted as the "bad guy." Although this may not happen as often as it once did — we are trying to teach acceptance, tolerance, and equality in schools — the subtle implications remain and children are not immune to them.

To recapitulate, then, children witness a subtle act of stereotyping, or even a violent act, and may as a result place blame unfairly and incorrectly. Teachers can help to undo the contributory negative stereotyping by drawing attention to the situation and discussing the possible causes as well as the appropriate "children" behaviors — that is, not judging without evidence.

Teachers can help younger children (ages 6–9) learn about stereotyping from media violence. First, they can encourage them to draw a picture representing someone committing a violent act and a victim. They can then ask the children to describe who is usually shown as the perpetrator of a violent act and who, the victim. By bringing their attention to the stereotyping, teachers will assist the children in starting to see it for themselves.

With older children, teachers can ask questions that will lead them to discover the stereotyping. Here are some possible leading questions:

1. Why do newspapers often show a violent act on page 1?
2. When a movie about to be released has a trailer, it often features the most violent parts. Why do you think that is?
3. How do people react to violence in movies? on TV? in the news?
4. What sorts of people are often used in film to be the most violent? Describe a typical violent character.
5. How true is this depiction in real life? Can a little grandmother be violent? Why do filmmakers adopt these stereotypes?
6. What sorts of people are often depicted as victims of violence? Why do you think that is the case?
7. What do you think happens if you watch too much violence? (Desensitization)
8. When a movie or TV show uses a particular type of dress or "costume" to portray a "bad guy," how does this affect you? What stereotypes are being perpetuated?

There is a real danger of unconsciously perpetuating inaccurate ideas about people, groups, races, and genders. Children have limited experience with the world. It is my belief that if they are allowed to entertain incorrect or stereotypical images of others, they can grow up to be less accepting, less compassionate, and possibly less able to deal with acts of violence in adulthood. I know that teachers can, as part of a discussion about a tough topic based on a violent act, point out possible situations of stereotyping and negate them.

Ideas such as those in the Formula Five below can be shared and multicultural activities, encouraged. Teachers can use acts of violence to teach anti-stereotyping. Doing so does not have to be difficult or even time consuming. Simply accept that the students have witnessed an uncomfortable situation from which they could easily stereotype a group, race, culture, or gender. Hold a discussion that includes the five points of the following Formula Five.

Formula Five: Teaching Anti-stereotyping from Violent Acts

Small groups do not represent the whole.
All people are basically the same.
We live in a mixed-culture mosaic.
Honor all cultures through cross-cultural activities.
Respect different points of view.

Small groups do not represent the whole. Point out that the people who have presumably committed a violent act do not represent *all* people of that race (group, gender, etc.) There are many Arabic children in our schools. They are not at all alike and should not be compared to the people suspected in the 9-11 tragedy. Invite kids to think of ways that familiar stereotypes, not necessarily just those associated with violence, are overruled right there in their school or community. Examples:

- All black people are athletic: In our class, Brandon, an African-American boy, hates sports and is great in the Drama Club.
- People who wear glasses and read a lot are nerds: Justine wears glasses and loves to read, but she is also popular and is captain of the girls' soccer team.
- Jocks are good looking, athletic, and dumb: Karl is a jock and he gets straight A's in every subject.

Discussion such as this can be directed towards any disturbing acts of violence with the caution to be very careful to avoid stereotyping.

All people are basically the same. Point out that in every group or culture, there are both good and bad people, but that all of them have families just like we do. All people are basically the same. Examples:

- The children in countries at war are just as frightened for their families as we would be if armed soldiers were roaming our streets.
- No one wants to live in poverty or fear.
- No one wants to feel hungry all the time and have to dig through garbage for food.

We live in a mixed-culture mosaic. Point out that children of other cultures attending our schools are not responsible for acts carried out by adults living in their homelands and that these children are just as vulnerable and frightened by acts of violence as we are. Help students to develop empathy for these other children. Remind them that we live in a mixed-culture mosaic, and remember to discuss all the positive ramifications of that. Examples:

- Foods and meals that originated in other cultures (e.g., curry)
- Entertainment from other cultures (e.g., Grass Dance by Aboriginal men)
- Special holidays and celebrations (e.g., Chinese New Year)

Honor all cultures through cross-cultural activities. Involve students in many cross-cultural activities as a regular part of the curriculum — teachers today are very familiar with this concept and are extremely careful to honor all cultures. You might arrange for

- guest speakers from other cultures talking about their homelands and cultures
- study and appreciation of special days and celebrations of various cultures (e.g., Ramadan, Chinese Lantern Festival)
- availability of free picture and chapter books from different cultures

Encourage different points of view. Encourage students to adopt the points of view of children from other countries, cultures, or socio-economic levels. Cite a situation, as in the examples following, and invite students to put themselves into the shoes of that child to think, feel, and act as he or she would. Examples:

- Afghan children may fear Western soldiers serving in their country, even though their relatives may be foreign soldiers we fear.
- Children who have immigrated to Canada may have family members, such as grandparents, still living in their homelands.
- A child from a far country whose ethnic beliefs decree that he or she wear a particular form of dress, such as a sari, has to mix daily with North American children.

Stereotyping and Cultural Dress
There is much confusion in the public mind about turbans and terrorists. Teachers can, and should, directly address this matter through class discussion or students' research. These important points should be made:

- Males in Sikh families are required to wear turbans, called "dastars."
- Men of many Islamic cultures wear forms of turbans; these differ from the turbans worn by Sikhs.
- Hindus often wear a head covering similar to the Sikh turban — a "puggaree."
- The 1985 Air India crash was caused by turban-wearing terrorists; 9-11 and the July 2005 bombings in London, England, were not.
- A turban is a form of cultural dress, not a symbol of terrorism.

The Dragon and the Mouse is a picture book about a mouse that is abused emotionally, physically, mentally, and socially by the dragon he lives with. Eventually he leaves but remains friends with the dragon. (This book is available only from Touchstone Enterprise, 2108 South University Drive Fargo, ND 58103 701 237-4742.)

Good Reads

A Terrible Thing Happened: A Story for Children Who Have Witnessed Violence or Trauma by Margaret M. Holmes (illustrated by Cary Pillo)

A Safe Place by Maxine Trottier (illustrated by Judith Friedman) (a story about domestic violence)

Please Tell!: A Child's Story About Sexual Abuse by Jessie Ottenweller (Early Steps)

The Dragon and the Mouse: About Living with Emotional, Physical and Mental Abuse by Steven Timm

Leo the Lop by Stephen Cosgrove (illustrated by Robin James) (Serendipity Books)

No Shame, No Fear by Ann Turnbull (a chapter book)

Witnessing Depressing or Cruel Situations

Here, I am not referring to the extreme violent acts discussed in the previous section, but rather to the upsetting, depressing situations children witness not only in Third World countries but also at home. Situations include famine and extreme poverty; horrific deaths due to natural disasters such as floods, hurricanes, tidal waves or storms; cruel treatment of females by Iraqi males; and rampant diseases, such as HIV, smallpox, and flu. Given the technology together with the aggressive media, children are more exposed to these situations than ever before, and that exposure can cause problems. Consider the following questions and statements that teachers have shared with me.

- "Teacher, why do those kids have such big bellies and such sad eyes? Don't they have mommies?" (Sarah, Grade 2)
- "I hate that we have so much food and all those people are starving. That's not fair." (Denice, Grade 8)
- "Do you know what they do to girls in Iraq? It's horrible. Why doesn't our government do something?" (Allie, Grade 9)
- "I just feel like crying when I see those people living in those tent things. What do they do? What do they eat? Why did we have to bomb them?" (Joel, Grade 5)
- "If I save half my lunch, can we sent it to those kids?" (Jason, Grade 1)
- "What if we all get sick and die? I saw on TV that everyone is getting sick and kids are dying. I don't want to die." (Sal, Grade 3)
- "Can we get a big wave here, too? I saw all those houses getting washed away. There were people in them too. I saw one guy . . . If it rains hard here, will we get a big wave too?" (Kelly, Grade 2)

These are real concerns attached to genuine sadness from real children, whose real teachers had to scramble for ways to handle the concerns. Although fear is still a prime factor, these concerns contain more sadness for the people suffering than those tied to violent acts, and so can be handled a bit differently.

Children feel the pain of people suffering. They want to help but often feel helpless. Some children even harbor feelings of guilt because they "have so much" while others have nothing. Young children tend to be primarily egotistical; they are worried about themselves and their immediate families. Because they don't understand why so many Third World children are experiencing hunger, disease, fear of bombs, or war, they worry that similar things might happen to them too. I refer to these younger children as the "me-mine" group.

Children of about ages 8 to 12 tend to be more aware of the needs of the others who are struggling. They are concerned with fairness and with helping, although they have no idea how to help. I refer to this group as the "Fair-share-care" group. They often shed copious tears for the children they see suffering.

The adolescents have an amazing social conscience, so much so that they readily take on causes, often without enough planning and pre-thought to make them successful. They are militant about their desire to "save" the world and are quick to express dislike of world leaders for not helping. Teachers must take into account all these levels of students' concerns when dealing with children who are upset by world catastrophes. Here are some ideas that should help.

Discuss and inquire.
Express feelings.
State the obvious — provide facts.
Channel anger.
Redirect personal options.

Formula Five: Helping Kids Deal with World Sorrows

Discuss and inquire. Lead a class discussion about a relevant trouble or situation that is concerning the students. Be prepared to provide information only as needed. Attempt to find out how much the students already know, to fill in the blanks as necessary, and to point out incorrect information they may have. Depending on the ages of the students, more or less information will be provided by them. Accept what they give. At this stage you are gathering information.

Express feelings. Disclose your own feelings about the situation. Doing so opens doors for kids to express their feelings. Accept all feelings. Use simple commands that allow kids to agree or disagree by simply raising hands: "Raise your hand if you, like Kelly, think this is a frightening thing." Help them to put their strong feelings into words by paraphrasing what they say and substituting other words where appropriate: "You said you feel bad. I think you mean very upset." However, avoid putting words into kids' mouths: "You are so quiet I think you must be furious."

State the obvious — provide facts. Specifically say what is terrible or wrong. For example, about children who are starving in Africa, you might say, ". . . is a tragedy, and people everywhere feel sad about it." There is absolutely no point in sugar-coating information. Students will know if you are lying and if you do, they will distrust you in the future. When they ask, tell them the basic facts, whether these pertain to deaths from a storm, number of people suffering from a disease, or whatever. Don't let the students embellish or make the situation worse than it is, but also don't let them downplay it. Facts are facts. Tell the truth and provide accurate information, the amount of which will depend on the ages of the students.

Channel anger. Many students will feel a sense of anger at the situation; they are empathizing with others and fail to understand why our world should "be so mean." Tell them that anger is normal and that being angry at a certain situation is normal; then, attempt to channel that anger into some activity, not at everyone in general. Feeling helpless in these situations often fuels the fire for children to be angry, so helping them find a constructive activity will be helpful. Examples of constructive activities are included in "Liberating activities," pages 24–25, especially numbers 3, 5, 6, and 11.

Redirect personal options. Talk about what the kids can do to deal with their feelings about a bad situation. Perhaps they can journal, draw, or have small-group discussions. Help kids to find comfort in the familiar and predictable by returning to what I call a "comfort food activity." Just as certain foods have become known as comfort foods for the sense of well-being associated with them, certain in-class activities have the same general "feel." The activities will differ from class to class, but a few I have found to be comforting to students include drawing to classical music at low volume, chanting, listening to a story read by the teacher, going for a nature walk, or taking part in a seated visualization activity, such as Hug-a-Tree. These are calming activities intended to help reduce the anger children feel.

Hug-a-Tree
Students close their eyes. They imagine hugging a tree, feeling, smelling, sensing the solidity of the trunk, and gaining a sense of oneness, or grounding.

Easy Accessibility of Drugs and Alcohol

Sometimes, we get so caught up in worrying about what our students will be tomorrow that we forget to appreciate who they are today. We miss important cues about their welfare. As significant adults, we fail to see what's right in front of us. I am referring to today's troubles with drug and alcohol abuse.

I know many elementary school teachers who believe their students are too young to be affected by use of drugs and alcohol. These teachers believe, wrongly, in the innocence and naivety of their charges. Like ostriches, they are hiding their heads in the sand while more young children are being exposed or are even becoming addicted to these harmful products. Why?

Once again, the media must take some of the blame; almost everywhere kids look, using drugs and alcohol is made to look cool. In addition, the prevalence of over-the-counter as well as prescription drugs in most medicine cabinets sends the message that drugs are okay, even helpful. Finally, peer pressure may work to emphasize that the "in" crowd uses drugs or alcohol. Children are easily confused and certainly curious. National studies show that curiosity about drugs and alcohol can start as young as age 5, that alcohol use can start as young as age 11, and use of marijuana can start as young as age 12 (talkingwithkids.org). Elementary teachers: Those are your students.

Unfortunately, one big trouble today is easy accessibility to these harmful substances. Dealers know how vulnerable young people are; they work hard to "catch" them and draw them into their webs. In some neighborhoods, young dealers have been spotted dealing right on children's playgrounds. (See the anecdote at left.)

Junior high and high schools are frequented by dealers and sellers even more often. If this is such a problem in today's troubled world, what can mere teachers do to help? Luckily, quite a bit. Although parents are the first line of attack where alcohol or drugs are concerned, they are often at a loss as to what to do. Sometimes, they turn to the teacher for advice, and sometimes the teacher has little to offer. At the least, if the teacher believes a child is using drugs or drinking, he should contact both the school counselor and the parents. Some interventions, however, can take place in a classroom, and with permission from parents and principal, with an entire class. These are outlined in the Formula Five on the next page.

A 13-year-old told me in all sincerity that when he wanted to "use," all he had to do was "call Bill" (apparently not his real name) and someone would make a delivery to the alley behind his house. "I'd just take out the garbage," he confided, "and give him some money that I told my mom I needed for school." It's that easy.

Discuss from the "I" perspective.
Listen carefully.
Provide age-appropriate information.
Role-play.
Be a good model with a zero tolerance position.

Good Idea

Break the class into random groups and have each group prepare a presentation titled "Ways to Feel Good." Group options include making a report, doing a skit, creating a poster, and telling a story. All ideas presented should be alternatives to using drugs or drinking alcoholic beverages.

Good Reads

Too Cool for Drugs by Sharon Scott and Wayne Hindmarsh (illustrated by George Phillips)

My Big Sister Takes Drugs by Judith Vigna

Jimmie Boogie Learns About Smoking (3d edition) by Tim Brenneman

Ned Learns to Say No: A Lesson About Drugs by Ron Madison

The Berenstain Bears and the Drug-Free Zone by Stan Berenstain

The Addiction Monster and the Square Cat by Sheryl Letzgus McGinnis

Formula Five: Dealing with Drugs and Alcohol

Discuss from the "I" perspective. Carefully open the discussion in such a way as to provide enough comfort that children will feel free to disclose and ask questions. The opening statements should define the concern clearly and provide your personal stance. Example: "I want us to talk together about a serious topic, one that is causing me great unhappiness and worry. I'm talking about drinking [or drugs]. I don't mean adult drinking, although that is troublesome too, but drinking by people your age." (Pause here for a few seconds. Kids may be shocked that you are broaching the subject so openly. Allow reaction time.) "I'd like you to help me understand why children [adolescents] like you would drink. Let's talk about this . . ." Usually, an opening like this will get them started, but if they are still reticent to talk, probe a bit: "Why does anyone drink? Think of someone who has had too much to drink. How did that person act? How is drinking harmful?"

Listen carefully. Teachers are talkers; sometimes the hardest thing for them to do is to listen carefully. Once the students start talking, pay close attention to everything that's said and not said, as well as to nonverbal cues. As soon as possible afterwards, jot down a few pertinent notes. You may need them later when talking to parents or professionals. Interject only for clarification.

Provide age-appropriate information. Attempt to summarize at least some of what has been said and then provide some honest, important, age-relevant information about the topic. What is provided will be based on instincts and knowledge of the group rather than on a set age, but an example for young children might be as follows: "That is something that can hurt our bodies. Let's think of better things that will help our bodies, such as . . ." With older students, the teacher might say, "Do you know how different types of liquor affect your bodies? Are you aware that alcohol can cause terrible damage to your liver? And what do you think it might do to your brain cells?" If students ask questions, answer honestly and succinctly; offer no more information than is necessary to answer the question. If you don't know the answer, say so and promise to find out and tell them later.

Role-play. Have students act out possible situations where they are faced with peers who are drinking or offering alcoholic drinks. Help them adopt a "just say no" approach and practise it. You might want to be the "opposition," the person who is trying hard to encourage the student to take a drink. Say and do everything you think another student might say and do; be relentless. Following the role play, come up with a list of alternatives to accepting a drink — words they could say, actions they could take. Create a group list, but have individual students copy the list in their books, arranging the order so that the action they record first is the first one they would take.

Be a good model with a zero tolerance position. Once I met a young student while shopping at a Safeway and she squealed with delight, "You shop at Safeway!" This was an *aha* experience for me. Often, our students see us as paragons of virtue, as beings who are not bothered by the mundane things in life like grocery shopping. Think how they would feel if they witnessed us drinking, using drugs, being drunk, or acting out of control? It is so important to maintain zero tolerance for alcohol or drugs, at least where our students are concerned. Of course, I am not suggesting we never take a sip of alcohol or down a couple of Tylenol. All I am saying is that while in control of a classroom, we speak of and believe in zero tolerance. It is also important to help students understand that there are other ways to feel good, to make friends, to boost self-confidence, and to have fun.

CHAPTER 3

Concerning Children of the New Decade

"The child must know that he is a miracle, that since the beginning of the world there hasn't been, and until the end of the world there will not be, another child like him."
— Pablo Casals

Children, students, the young people who will someday take over the world with all its troubles and turmoil, the little people who make up 33 percent of our population and 100 percent of our future, are the focus of this section. Of course, the entire book is dedicated to their ultimate welfare, but this chapter, in particular, will offer suggestions for helping them with problems that seem specific to this decade. Every child, after all, is a unique expression of life and will leave some sort of contribution to humanity. Teachers, through their awareness of and attention to current problems facing their students, can help their students' contributions to be as positive as possible.

Not so many years ago I recall wondering how teachers could best respond to explicit questions about sex and sexuality. I am rather amazed that this matter seems to be a concern of the past. It has been replaced by the terrors children have about the state of the world in which they live. The problem for teachers remains the same, however: how to respond.

Every situation is different. The ages and abilities of the children must be considered, as well as the question content, but unlike the sex-based questions, the teacher cannot simply say, "Ask your parents" or "I'll get back to you on that after I speak to the counselor." Today's questions call for today-answers. As with other components of *Teaching in Troubled Times*, the issues here are huge, so much so that any one of them could easily fill a book. As with the other components, I have attempted to condense and prioritize ideas so that the busy teacher can quickly locate and use simple, specific, and effective strategies.

Mary McLeod Bethune, an American educator, said, "We have a powerful potential in our youth, and we must have the courage to change old ideas and practices so that we may direct their power toward good ends." Teachers already know that; what they may not be so comfortable with are the means to those ends. Teachers also know that they are culpable if they ignore the hot topics, the worried queries, or the sensitive issues. Somehow, they must meet the challenges of teaching in today's world regardless of how daunting and frightening the world may be and impel their students into an unknown future. They want to provide for these young people experiences, challenges, and excellent instruction. They want to give them as many tools for self-efficiency as possible. They want to be able to recognize their fears, their worries, and their questions and turn them into teachable moments and chances for self-discovery. No small task. No easy way out. No problem for all the great teachers reading this book.

I have selected four components for this chapter on children in today's troubled world, each one because it appears to be a current problem. Whether that's because of the chaotic condition of our world, the rampant explosion of technology, the economic meltdown with its myriad problems and so on, I don't know.

What I do know is that students are exhibiting more and more problems in these areas, and consequently creating difficult and demanding realities for teachers. The four areas that represent the most prevalent problems as suggested to me by teachers are as follows: (1) discovery of self, (2) socialization of self, (3) independence of self, and (4) wellness of self, which encompasses nutrition and fitness.

Discovery of Self in a Confusing Environment

How well do you know yourself? In this troubled and chaotic world, what part do or will you play? Where are you going? What do you want to do? **Who are you?**

In answer to the last question above, most of us will answer with our names and professions. "I'm Kathy Paterson, a teacher." But there is so much more to each of us, so many individualities, idiosyncrasies, hidden traits and talents, wants and desires, needs and dreams . . . so many components to every human being that I doubt many of us truly know exactly who we are. Hence the question, *How **well** do you know yourself?*

At a school track meet I witnessed the following interaction. One of the runners, an attractive adolescent who had just won her race, was crouched on the grass beside the wheelchair of another student, a girl with a twisted body and beatific smile.

"Don't you feel bad that you can't run too? Be a part of the meet like everyone else?" the runner asked, not unkindly.

"No," the girl in the wheelchair replied. "Not at all. I know that I have spina bifida and I know that people with crippled spines like mine can't take part in track meets, so I don't expect myself to do that and I don't feel bad. And actually, I'm lucky. I don't have any abnormalities in my brain — lots of people with this disease do, you know — and so I can totally enjoy watching you run."

When the runner looked shocked, the girl laughed and added, "It's all about knowing yourself . . ."

The conversation didn't end there, but for the purposes of this book it did.

Knowing yourself! Sounds easy, but for many of us, especially children, it is not. And for reasons mixed and many, this awareness of self is fighting for time in the lives of children today — and losing! I submit that children today are considerably less aware of who and what they are, where they are going, and what they can and want to do. This lack of self-awareness is a problem for teachers.

The tenet *Know thyself* was originally attributed to Greek philosophers long ago. It can, however, be considered the basis of human growth and development, the discovery and understanding of self and all that that entails, as much today as in the past. And I firmly believe that children need to be instructed in this exploration of self, need to be tutored to correctly learn about themselves, need to be coached in their ongoing quests for self-awareness.

Not relevant, you might think, unimportant based on the already overwhelming curriculum content I'm responsible to teach.

Think of the child who believes, because Grandma told her so, that she can dance like a "fairy," but who is teased relentlessly by peers for her awkward movements. Or, think of the child who desires to be a professional basketball player but who will never be tall enough to be a viable contender, and yet is encouraged by well-meaning adults to follow his dream.

On the other hand, consider the child who *does* have a talent or skill, but who seems unaware of it or unable to accept it. For instance, a girl is excellent at mathematics, but perhaps because she feels she will be ostracized by peers if she exhibits this skill, she refuses to acknowledge it and doesn't excel in the subject. Or consider the boy who is a natural public speaker yet shies away from any class activity that involves speaking to an audience because he feels incapable. Each case represents an error in awareness of self. Each case represents a failure to accurately self-discover. Each case leads to an unhappy child.

Of course, I'm not negating in *any* way the amazing successes people have had in the face of adversity. Terry Fox, for example, ran across Canada with one leg, there are quadriplegic artists who manipulate paint brushes with their mouths, and hundreds of athletes confined to wheelchairs take part in competitive games. The list is endless, suggesting that adults should never discourage children from trying to excel because everywhere they look, examples of excelling-in-spite-of-a-limitation abound. The point I am trying to make is that everyone, even a person with special challenges, needs to begin with a sound and accurate understanding of self. This is where teaching comes into play, and that is the focus of this chapter.

Show me a teacher who cares about students, who appreciates the need for them to be independent, self-confident, and successful in life, and I'll show you a teacher who wants to lead students on the path of self-discovery.

The Formula Five below outlines important areas to address when helping students learn about themselves. Each teaching suggestion has been effectively tested. Keep in mind that the goal here is to develop or improve upon an awareness of self. These suggestions do not need to be discussed or presented in any specific sequence. They are quick and ready tasks that can be introduced within the curriculum of most subjects to encourage student self-discovery.

Formula Five: Areas of Self-Awareness

Strengths and weaknesses. Well into adolescence many students have difficulty identifying their personal strengths and weaknesses. Teachers can help by providing open-ended statements, such as "I am good at . . ." or "I have trouble with . . . ," and then following with small-group or one-on-one discussions. In addition, there are specific teacher tips, including these:

- Avoid false praise. Help the student understand a strength or weakness by specifically describing it for him: "You have trouble with math because you don't know your times tables . . ."
- Be optimistic when discussing a weakness and use specific words. Use positive terms and leave the child with a strategy for improvement or an alternative idea. For example, for a weak student in physical education say, "You have a weakness in stamina — that means you can't keep up for very long. But this will get better if you . . ."
- Balance a weakness with a strength. "You have difficulty singing a solo, but you can play the piano beautifully."
- Remind the child that everyone has weaknesses and that makes us normal. If possible, help the child find a way to compensate for or deal with an identified weakness.
- Think like a child when discussing weaknesses. In other words, use mind pictures and analogies when possible. Rather than telling a seven-year-old she has a weakness in doing division, say: "You know how when your mom is baking a cake, if she leaves out one ingredient, say, the sugar, the cake won't turn out right? Well, you've left out one ingredient for doing division. You are not sure of

Another word of support for a teacher-encouraged pursuit of self-discovery:

I asked a lovely woman of 100 plus years if she could live her life over again, would she do anything differently. She replied, "Oh certainly, dear. I'd take the time to find out who I really was before I was all grown up and it was too late."

Enough said.

Strengths and weaknesses.
Physical body image.
Personality.
Likes and interests.
Future me.

your times tables and that's making your answers not turn out right. We can fix this by . . ."

Physical body image. It's believed that a child's body image is determined by age six, so school is an excellent place to reinforce positive body image. Body image has a huge effect on behavior, so it follows that an incorrect body image could well result in less-than-stellar behaviors. An example would be the young girls in Grade 3 or 4 who refuse to eat so that they can look like the models in magazines. A Grade 3 girl was overheard saying to a peer, "I'm dumb. I'm not pretty like Sylvia so I'm stupid." Already at age seven, she was equating looks with ability.

Teachers can employ any of the following tips to promote students developing accurate body images and awareness of self.

- Talk about realistic norms in height, weight, eye colors, hair color, and so on.
- Promote acceptance of all people, regardless of size, color, beauty (according to cultural norms), and so on. For example, whenever possible, verbalize acceptance and in the classroom have resources celebrating all body types — *No Body's Perfect: Stories by Teens About Body Image, Self-Acceptance and the Search for Identity* by Kimberly Kirberger is a good example.
- Help students develop an accurate awareness of their own bodies by providing assignments that require them to really look at themselves both as parts (e.g., hands, fingers, feet) and as wholes.
- If you have access to a digital camera, take full facial photos of the students, download to your computer, and print off black-and-white copies. These will provide students with accurate visuals of their facial shapes, eyes, noses, and so on. Be sure to delete the downloads and provide the prints only to the students.
- Constantly promote the idea that beauty is not only an outer characteristic but an inner one. Someone can still be beautiful, loved, admired, and respected, and have a large nose. In any event, ideas of beauty and of normalcy, which is tied to it, change from decade to decade, culture to culture. There really is no "normal." The softer, rounded body-type perceived as perfection in the sixteenth century is far from today's svelte, fit image of perfection. Discussing with students the concept of uniqueness, and pointing out how they should appreciate the exceptional as well as the "normal" in a physical characteristic or personal trait is a good idea.

Good Idea

Provide small hand mirrors and have students illustrate, cartoon style if they want, or write a description of different body parts. Point out how the illustration or description should "be exactly like you." For example, if someone has a scar on a leg, the child should draw a scar on the leg. Sometimes, this exercise can bring light to children's mistakes in physical body image. For example, a child in a wheelchair who drew himself running ended up visiting the school counselor for help with accepting his condition. As a rule, any activity that requires students to carefully examine their physical selves is a powerful learning tool.

Good Idea

Post images of beauty from other cultures, perhaps photos showing people with elongated earlobes or paintings of heavy Rubenesque women, and invite students to add to the collection if they come across other examples. This exercise opens their eyes to the concept of beauty as transient and culturally biased.

Students can use the "Funny Faces" technique with animal shapes, stickmen, monsters, and more.

"Funny Faces" Motivator

The purpose is to point out how all faces are different and special through a game activity where partners work together to create funny or ridiculous faces.

1. Students first fold a blank page lengthwise (vertically). Student *A* then begins drawing a half-face on one side of the paper, making sure her lines go right to the fold. While *A* is drawing, *B* has closed eyes.

With paper folded, *B* draws face, starting and stopping at the fold.

fold

A draws this side with paper folded, and marks top and bottom of the face (▬).

2. The teacher as timekeeper indicates when every 15 seconds has passed, perhaps saying, "Change." On the teacher's cue, *A* turns the page over and *B* draws, without knowing where *A*'s lines are.
3. The activity continues in this manner for 3 or 4 minutes; then, the teacher invites the students to open the pages out flat and admire their creations. They can name their faces and share with peers.

Personality. As much as we'd like to believe otherwise, children's physical characteristics have an effect on their personalities. Take, for example, the short, pudgy boy who longs to be an athlete, with the result being a snarly, disruptive personality. The struggle between what he is and what he wants to be causes unrest and anger.

In class encourage students to keep a record of things they do that suggest a personality trait: "I stopped to help Mrs. X so I think I am kind and helpful." It doesn't matter whether the description of their personality trait(s) is correct: the main thing is that they begin to be aware of what they do and why they do it.

It's also good to have children write descriptions of their personalities together with what they would like to change, if anything, and how they think they might go about that. Remember that this is an exercise in self-discovery, so encourage and reinforce any *ahas*.

You can reinforce the individual personalities of your students in these ways:

- Emphasize that there are no good or bad personality types; all people are unique, and all have special talents and gifts.
- Remember to treat all students equally. Children's personalities are in formation when they are in your class; contribute to the positive part of that formation by showing respect for all.
- Understand your own personality type and disclose as much as you feel comfortable with the students: "I am the kind of person who hates to be . . . It makes me grumpy."

Self-Discovery Charts: A Personality-Promoting Strategy

This fun activity for children helps them to look closely at their inner selves, their personalities. Present the idea of a self-discovery chart by drawing a horizontal line on the board with familiar, related concepts, such as happy and sad, printed at opposite ends. Draw a vertical line in the middle of the horizontal line. Write "average" right on top of the vertical line to indicate that the centre point shows an average degree of that feeling. Now mark an X somewhere on the horizontal line to indicate how you *generally* feel. Explain this to the students: "Most of the time I am happy so I put the X here. I can't put it all the way to the right because I'm not *always* happy."

Provide students with two copies of the chart. One they fill in according to how they see themselves; the other they fill in by asking two or three people for their input. These responses should be marked in different colors. For example, a mother's responses might be red X's and a friend's, orange, and so on.

Have students compare all the responses and come up with a written description of their general demeanors or personalities based on how they see themselves as well as how others see them.

Possible Self-Discovery Chart Scales:

happy	sad
outgoing	reserved
forgiving	blaming
quiet	talkative
good listener	poor listener
thoughtful	selfish

Good Idea

Invite students to compare their lists of interests with peers, looking for someone who has similar likes or interests that they didn't previously know about. They then record this information in journals: "I found out that both John and I like . . ."

Likes and interests. This area changes daily, even hourly, with children, but nonetheless is an important part of self-awareness. Some children have trouble identifying interests. Teachers can help by providing a basic umbrella theme list such as "games, sports, snacks, drinks, television shows, books, colors, after-school activities, places" and so on. In this way, students can focus on a specific area and make a choice as to what they like and where their interests lie. I remember one young man who joyfully clapped his hands when he had completed an "Interests" list. When I asked for an explanation, he said, "I never knew how much I was interested in. Boy! Look at this list! And I never knew I liked talking to Granddad on the phone so much until I put it on this list. I can do just about anything when I grow up, hey?"

Future me. Invite children to look at themselves 10 or 20 years hence. They can illustrate or write about who, what, and where they think they will be in the future. They love to fantasize about the future. This activity tends to be a favorite part of a self-discovery search.

Another idea is to identify who or where they want to be, then list some actions they will have to take to get there. This activity works well with older children, many of whom are already gearing school for their futures. For those who have no idea what they want to do, this task can be enlightening as it starts them thinking that their futures are within their control. At the very least, making personal future predictions is a viable tool for self-discovery.

An alternative to this activity is Future You/Future Me: In this task, students work in pairs, interviewing each other to glean previously unfamiliar facts or information, then writing a short biography of the partner and adding a "future you" section in which the students make predictions about each other based on what they know. If the task evolves into a Language Arts activity and students give permission, students can present their final projects.

Here's an example of a prediction a Grade 6 student made, based on the responses to her questions. I have shortened it but left enough for clarification of the concept.

Good Idea

Sometimes, children present ideas about their future selves that are unrealistic or at least improbable (e.g., the large child who sees himself becoming a racehorse jockey). When students are fantasizing their futures and you think it would be constructive to point out that not all things are possible, set the impossible task: Have students draw a big "6" in the air with their fingers. At the same time, challenge them to make clockwise circles with a foot. If you first ask whether they think they can do this, most will say yes. It is, however, impossible to make the hand move counterclockwise (the "6") while the foot is moving clockwise. Conclusion? Some things are impossible.

Q: What do you like to do best on weekends?
A: Go to the library and look up stuff about the ocean and ocean animals.
Q: Do you have a pet?
A: No, but I'd like to have a pet dolphin.
Q: Where have you traveled to that you really liked?
A: San Diego. We went to the zoo there and Marine Land. The whales were so amazing. And the dolphins and all the beautiful underwater sea plants.

Paragraph from final report:
Vicky will be a famous oceanographer. She will travel the world examining ocean life and testing oceans for pollution. She will write a book about this that will make her millions but she'll put the money into cleaning up the oceans . . .

Interesting note: Vicky did indeed go on to study at The School of Earth and Ocean Studies at the University of Victoria, British Columbia.

Ideas for Promoting Student Self-Awareness Within Existing Curriculum

Since all teachers are already swamped with curriculum, they may be reluctant to inject any more content into their days. Consequently, I have suggested a number of practical ways to do this, while still striving to meet the mandated curriculum.

- *Animals Now & Then:* Ask students to think of the animal they are most like at present. Tell them to choose not just because they like a particular animal but according to some behavior or appearance of that creature. "I'm a monkey because I like to climb trees, get into trouble, and act silly." Have them illustrate or write about their choices. Then ask what animal they might be in 10 or 20 years, using the same criteria as before. Some children keep the same animal; if so, they need to justify their reasons. "I'm still a monkey because I don't want to grow up." Usually, they choose a different animal and their reasons are quite amazing. This thought-provoking activity encourages thinking about the future.

    Curriculum Connections: Science, Language Arts, Art

- *The Self-Discovery Book:* Give each student (or ask them to provide) a book, duo-tang, or folder in which they will keep all their self-discovery materials, such as those from the five parts of the preceding Formula Five. This book will not only be a great source of potential writing projects but can serve as a catalyst at parent–teacher conferences and even as a possible source of formative evaluation — I avoid providing summative evaluations on these books.

    I prefer a book that has a folder-type jacket where students can put bits and pieces of paper, pictures, and so on that relate to their self-discovery. If this is not possible, tape a large brown envelope inside the back cover of the writing book. Keep these books all in one place (e.g., a special tub in the room) where students can easily find them.

    This Self-Discovery Book is the student's personal property and should be shared but not marked; however, the contents might be used for a different project, such as a writing task or a science experiment, and that assignment could be evaluated.

    Curriculum Connections: Language Arts, Health, Art, Social Studies

- *Friday Feature:* Another idea for use of the contents of this book is to create a "Friday Unit." All teachers are only too familiar with "Friday funk" — that never-ending period of time from lunch to home time on Friday afternoons. It seems students leave by 1 p.m. on Fridays; the older the students, the more they fade into daydreams for this final part of the school week. Perhaps a different sort of unit — a unit that is motivating because it is entirely about the students, allows them to learn about themselves in a unique manner, and whose only evaluation is the inherent awareness of self — will be just the thing to relieve Friday doldrums. I suggest selecting parts or all of the contents of this book, introducing the Self-Discovery Books, and establishing a time each Friday for self-discovery.

    Curriculum Connections: Language Arts, Health, Art, Social Studies

- *Spontaneous Selections:* Some days just don't work according to plan and everything seems to go wrong. The next time this happens, I suggest stopping everything else, announcing to the class that they are going to find out something important about themselves, probably something they didn't already know, and jump right into any lesson you choose. With this approach, no Self-Discovery Book is established (although you may find you need one) and the lesson is free-standing. Its inherent motivation — namely, that it's specific to each child — allows it to proceed easily.

  Curriculum Connections: Language Arts, Health, Art, Social Studies

- *Home Study:* Another way to use the personal information gathered during any self-discovery activity (although it is not my favorite way) is to consider it as a home study unit. Sometimes, students are away from school for extended periods (due to illness, strikes, school closures, or family vacations) and teachers want to assign a study unit that will connect to and expand upon regular in-class work, and yet be highly motivating. Again, since the topics covered in this book are intrinsically motivating, a mini self-discovery unit would be perfect. You may want to limit the unit to any one of the major categories (e.g., physical body) and provide a breakdown (e.g., parts of the face, hands, feet, body) as well as an explanation and your expectations.

  Curriculum Connections: Language Arts, Art

- *Needed Nuggets:* A final suggestion for use of a quick self-discovery lesson is what I refer to as "needed nuggets," or specific lessons used when an occasion prompts or a need is indicated. An example of this would be when a piece of literature in Language Arts involves a protagonist who suffers hate and a need for revenge; you could quickly pull out and use part or whole of the "Personality" section of self-discovery. Then you could invite students to compare their personalities to that of the protagonist, or ask them to write a description of the protagonist's personality based on what they have read.

  Curriculum Connections: Language Arts, Health, Art, Social Studies, Mathematics, Science (charts and comparisons)

- *Advertising Deconstruction:* Most teachers talk to their students about the power of advertising; indeed, close examination of advertisements, together with the various advertising techniques they use — glittering generalities, famous person endorsements, and so on — are components of the Language Arts curriculum. The idea of ad deconstruction, however, may be new. To do this, you, as the teacher, talk in the manner of a "think-aloud" to the advertisement, denouncing something about the physicality of the characters involved. We are aware that most ads, particularly those addressed to young people, use waif thin models with impossibly shiny hair and porcelain skin. We are also aware that these photographs have been retouched, air blown, and Photoshopped until they are perfect. And, unfortunately, we know that young people want to be, long to be, and try to be like the models. Herein lies the problem for fragile, developing self-concepts. So, you "talk" to the ads in such a way that the students see what you see. You might say:

  "You are so skinny you look foolish."
  "I'm so glad none of my students looks like you because I think you look unhealthy and frail."
  "Thank goodness I don't know girls who dress like that."

"I wonder what they put on your hair to make it look so unnaturally shiny? Maybe wax. Ug!"

The goal is to point out how outrageous and silly some of the ads are. By doing this you can, at the same time, provide credence for more "normal" appearances. Taking this approach seems to work much better than just telling the students how you feel.

Curriculum Connections: Language Arts, Art, Mathematics, Science

- *Formula Five — All About Me:* The following Formula Five helps students realize that they are more than physical bodies, smiling students, or trusting friends — they have a great many facets. By having them complete the Formula Five and then return to it occasionally to add or delete words, the teacher will give students one more tool for self-awareness.

Curriculum Connections: Language Arts, Social Studies, Health, Physical Education

A Attitude.
B Behavior.
C Compassion.
D Dependability.
E Effort.

Good Idea

Ask students if they have ever received a letter or card in the mail and how, given the billions of people in the world, it found them. They will talk of addresses. Draw to their attention the fact that a personal address is a perfect example of how unique each person is. The address eliminates and eliminates, from general (country) to more and more specific (city, street) until it identifies one distinctive person. This analogy helps children see how unique each of them truly is.

Formula Five: All About Me

This Formula Five is an acrostic using the first five letters of the alphabet in sequence, so students can recall it easily and enjoy working with it. They copy the acrostic and add words pertaining to themselves.

Attitude. What is my attitude? How do I feel about my family? my life in general? school . . .?

Behavior. How do I usually behave at home? in school? on the playground?

Compassion. How do I react to others? With caring? With sincere interest and concern?

Dependability. Am I dependable? Do I do what I say I am going to do? Do I keep secrets?

Effort. Do I try my best at school? in sports? Do I put effort into my . . .?

To promote self-discovery further, constantly remind students that each of them is unique, and happily so. What a boring world this would be were it otherwise! The "Same Make, Same Model" motivator focuses on this matter.

Same Make, Same Model Motivator

This activity aims to help students value individual uniqueness.

1. Have students stand and assume the forms of robots. Tell them they are all copies of one prototype robot and hence look and act in exactly the same manner.
2. Either the teacher or a chosen student is the number 1 robot, and all the others must do exactly as the number 1. Allow movement, robotic style, for a couple of minutes, and then return to desks.
3. Follow up with a discussion about what our world would be like if we were all exactly the same. Emphasize that our individual uniqueness is important.

Socialization of Self

The world has changed since we were kids. So much of what was true for us is no longer true, and we can't go back to old, comfortable ways of being, acting, or teaching. Today's children are raised on technology! Consider the Chinese proverb "One generation plants the trees; another gets the shade." Unfortunately, the trees our generation planted were not always good; many of them were the seeds of technology now run rampant to the point where our children, locked in the shade of what we have done, have forgotten how to play in the sun. This is a generalization, but unfortunately, it is also true for far too many young people today. Teachers everywhere bemoan the fact that their students have forgotten, or perhaps never learned, how to socialize. "They spend too much time, alone, in front of a television or computer, playing solitary games with a machine," one teacher told me, and all the others within earshot agreed. "They lack a sense of connection," another said.

It is not surprising that scientists are researching how video and computer games can affect the way children act and think. There are concerns about children not only becoming more violent but also becoming somewhat immune to violent acts. Consider the video games in which the more violent you are, the more points you accrue. Now imagine what this does to heart rate, to degree of tension, to the ability to feel compassion, and so on. Probably you are thinking, and correctly so, that none of this has been proven, and you are right, but the concern persists.

Then, consider the whole topical issue of "playing alone" versus "playing with others." This troublesome trend towards physical isolation is being encouraged by the proliferation of electronic devices. A 2006 issue of *Time* magazine reported that children, on average, spent six hours daily glued to some sort of isolating electronic device. I would guess that today the number of hours thus removed from face-to-face socialization has increased. Or what about the area of stereotyping, especially gender stereotyping, that is most certainly promoted by many video games? This, too, is a growing concern. Of course, not all poor socialization skills are the result of physical isolation, video games, or the witnessing of violent acts. There are many reasons, far too many for the scope of this book, for this crisis, and some children simply have more difficulty than others in learning how to get along. However, as with self-awareness, I contend, based on what I have seen and what teachers have shared with me, socialization skills appear to be weaker in today's children than in those of a decade ago, It is possible, therefore, poor socialization skills are another symptom of our troubled world. Teachers want to help deal with this issue; they can be the first line of attack.

Description of a well-socialized child

After asking a number of teachers what they thought to be a well-socialized child, I have come up with the following list. It is included here for reference only. Use it as you see fit, but keep in mind that the uniqueness of every child makes a list such as this less than comprehensive at best. A well-socialized child

- is liked by peers and teachers
- has one or two good friends, and many casual friends
- is respectful (not rude) to peers and adults
- displays poise in social situations: interacts well
- accepts responsibility
- generally has a pleasant demeanor
- is compassionate and helpful to others

Now that we have a better idea of what a well-socialized child looks like, how do we help our students, especially those "difficult" ones who constantly test teachers' patience, to become better socialized? Games, especially cooperative ones, are good socialization builders, but there are some less familiar activities that teachers can try, too. Some of these are outlined in the next section.

Top 10 Class Activities That Promote Socialization

1. *Helping Hands:* This is an all-year or ongoing activity to which a class must be thoroughly committed but which has amazing and positive results. Each student chooses someone to help, to be that person's "helping hands" for the entire school year or as much of it as is possible. The selected recipient can be an adult in the school (caretaker, secretary, counselor, volunteer), in the community (corner-store owner, senior, person with special needs, priest, young mother), or another child, preferably younger (different grade or school, neighboring Kindergarten). The recipient must agree to be visited by the Helping Hand at least once or twice a month. (The number of times will differ according to the teacher's wishes.) The visits will vary in duration, but each one will provide assistance of some sort to the recipient. For example, a Grade 5 student might fold laundry for a young mother, or a Grade 6 student might walk a senior's dog or cut his grass. The whole purpose of Helping Hands is to encourage socialization between the student and the recipient, a person with whom the student would not normally interact.

It is important that whenever possible, both parties write a few comments about the experience. Sometimes though, that may not be feasible. A Kindergarten student or a vision-impaired senior, for example, would not be able to write. In such instances, an illustration or a positive phone call to the teacher or supervisor would work fine. The point is to provide feedback for the student as well as for the teacher, as well as to encourage the recipient to acknowledge the act. After each Helping Hands visit, the recipient will also sign or even make an *X* in the Helping Hands Handbook, which can be any sort of scribbler, duo-tang, or notebook desired, or even a few single sheets stapled together.

After each agreed-upon time, student helpers can write about or illustrate their learning and note in what ways they feel they have improved their ability to socialize.

2. *Pick-a-Pal:* All teachers are familiar with the idea of pen pals for writing development. I suggest using this useful tool to further socialization skills. To do this, the students each pick someone they wouldn't normally socialize with after the teacher involves another class either in the school or in a different school (my preference). Before a pal is picked, students are given some rudimentary information about the other students, based on the Pick-a-Pal Questionnaire. They are then helped (teacher involvement) to pick a pal as different from themselves as possible. For instance, Joylene, a dancer with interests in figure skating, picks a girl with special needs who likes reading. Of course, it may not be possible for all children to be matched with their "opposites," but the idea is to avoid the children picking the same category of "pals" as usual. Both classes will complete the questionnaires; however, only the initiating class will make the pal choices. The receiving class will be given the information about their new pals following the selection process. If all works according to plan, the receiving class will be paired with "opposites" too.

Once pals have been picked, letter writing begins. It's amazing how children who would normally not pick each other become friends, hence improving their socialization skills.

Outline for Pick-a-Pal Questionnaire
(Note: Students can alter this as they see fit.)

Hi. My name is _____ and I want to be your pen pal. Please fill in the blanks below.
Favorite animal _____
Favorite sport _____
Favorite TV show or movie _____
Favorite food _____
What you like to do after school _____
What you like to do on weekends _____
Favorite school subject _____
Worst school subject _____
Pet peeve _____

3. *Random Acts of Socialization:* Borrowed from the idea of random acts of kindness, this concept is similar. After discussing how a well-socialized student behaves (see page 56), invite children to take part in random acts of socialization: to do things such as talking to someone they might not ordinarily speak to at recess, starting a friendly discussion with a neighbor or relative, chatting on the phone with a grandparent or someone who is ill, writing a note to someone to show you care. Brainstorm for little things the students can do that would

Good Idea

Invite students to keep a record of the acts of socialization on special pages in a journal where they jot down points. Students can return to those records occasionally for follow-up activities, such as "Share Care" discussions, where they talk about an act and explain the socialization involved, or writing assignments about a random act of socialization.

constitute acts of socialization. Of course these are, in fact, acts of kindness too, but that is unimportant here. The goal is to promote good socialization skills, and if that means acts of kindness — bonus!

4. *The Perfect Pal:* This is a favorite activity with many teachers, including me, and it can be used effectively with almost any concept in this book. I have chosen to include it here because it fits well with Pick-a-Pal. First, invite students to draw and write about the absolute perfect pal. They can use any technique that works for them, perhaps collage, painting, or sketching, together with lists of words and phrases that describe the perfect pal. Ask leading questions such as the following to get them thinking:

- What does the pal do when you talk? Cry? Get angry? Tell a fib?
- How does the pal act if you don't call? Get another friend? Call you?
- If you hurt the pal, what action can you expect in return?
- Does the pal have a specific appearance? Is so, what and why? If not, why?
- What does the pal like to do after school? in school? on weekends? on holidays?
- What do others think of your pal? What about adults? teachers? other kids?

Once they have clearly identified the characteristics of their perfect pals, something that may take more than one or two visits to the task, ask them to compare this picture to themselves. In other words, "How do you fit the description of a perfect pal?" Encourage honesty, but assure students that this assessment is not for "marks" but for self-development and determining how good they are at socialization. Their comparisons might be in graph or chart form, in writing using a comparative tool such as a Venn diagram or T-chart, in essay or paragraph form, or in another collage or illustration. The goal is to get students thinking about what kinds of images they give to the world and how good they are at being friends.

Smilerama Motivator

This activity promotes an awareness of the importance of smiles and works well in tandem with "Secret Smile."

Invite students to take part in a poster-making contest in which individuals or pairs find an interesting quotation about smiles or smiling, copy it on their poster paper, and illustrate it. (I find children enjoy this activity so much the contest aspect is not always necessary; however, for some students, "contest" implies working harder.) A favorite quotation of mine is the maxim "A smile confuses an approaching frown."

In encouraging a secret smile, be sure to reinforce that the child should not smile at a stranger who may present problems. While smiling at a senior in a home would be great, smiling at a stranger in a mall would be less so.

5. *Secret Smile:* A sincere smile works wonders: the value of that smile is immeasurable. When a child has difficulty socializing, encouraging him to give his "secret smile" can be very beneficial. The idea is to smile at someone he wouldn't usually pay any attention to.

A secret smile is saved for special people. With the child, identify who these might be (e.g., someone in class who looks upset, a child on the playground who looks lonely, a senior in a home or lodge, the school-bus driver, a grocery-store clerk). The idea is to encourage kids to use their smiles to brighten up the days of others, and by so doing, they will brighten up their own days and learn a little about positive socialization. Invite students to keep a journal of where and when they used their secret smiles, and what reactions they saw. By sharing these reactions with peers, positive socialization is reinforced. Often, children who don't socialize well, don't smile well either. It may be worth while discussing the difference between sincere smiles and false smiles.

Good Ideas

1. Smile at the class using your mouth only, maintaining a closed body position (arms crossed, standing stiffly). Ask the class if they trust your smile. Talk about where we see false smiles (perhaps on TV, family members, or teachers). You may want to look at pictures of smiles and judge the sincerity of the smiles. This is a fun, often eye-opening exercise for everyone.

2. Tell students to turn to a partner and decide who is *A* and who is *B*. Tell *B* to smile at *A*. Ask what happened. (*A* smiled back — it's hard not to.) Invite them to try *not* to return a genuine smile.

Good Reads

One Smile by Cindy McKinley
Muffin Dragon by Stephen Cosgrove (illustrated by Robin James) (Serendipity Books)
I Love It When You Smile by Sam McBratney
Never Smile at a Monkey: And 17 Other Important Things to Remember by Deborah Stevenson (a chapter book)

---

6. *Children's Literature:* I imagine all teachers are already aware of the importance of children's literature in teaching socialization skills, so I will mention it only briefly here. Good stories teach intrinsically by sharing examples of good and not-so-good behaviors that children can readily relate to. Post-reading discussions can bring to students' attention any specific skills the teacher wants to emphasize. When read aloud to adolescents — yes, they love being read to — with exaggerated eloquence and voice intonations, good picture books are excellent for introducing lessons on socialization skills.

7. *Role Playing:* Role playing potentially difficult socialization situations in the safety of the classroom is still one of the best ways to teach students about, or refresh their memories of, the better ways to behave with others. Experience has shown that if the teacher sets the stage by providing simple scenarios for the students to act out, more is learned than by leaving the choices entirely up to them. Break the class into groups of 3 to 5, and provide each group with two possible scenarios from which to choose their favorite. In this way, the groups still have a "choice." Allow about five minutes for them to devise a little improvisation based on the scenario. Remind them that they are trying to demonstrate good socialization behaviors, but that they can fill in whatever details they want to make the skit interesting. Although it's sometimes fun to have them act out the "bad" behaviors as a contrast, it becomes too tempting for some students to later mimic those behaviors rather than the positive ones. Be sure to revisit each skit and discuss the good behaviors and what else might work or not work.

Sample Scenarios:
- You are meeting a new student who is just coming to our school from a foreign country.
- You are at an adult gathering with your parents and an elderly woman is sitting all alone.
- In the playground, a lonely looking, younger student approaches you and asks you to play catch. You want to play with your own friends.
- At recess (or lunch break) your peer group sees an unfamiliar (or unpopular) student sitting alone crying.
- You witness two younger kids fighting, pushing, and shouting on the school grounds after school. No adults are around.

- You are invited to a party, but you don't know anyone else who's going. The person who invited you is not very popular, but you sort of like him (or her).
- Introduced to one of your mother's friend's children, you are expected to spend some time with them.

8. *Personal Pleasing Letters:* There are a couple of ways to handle this activity whereby students write positive, friendly letters or notes to others. The first way involves putting all the students' names into a hat and allowing random selection. Each student then writes a friendly letter to the person whose name was chosen. The letter must contain at least one thing the writer likes or appreciates about the person, as well as one skill or positive trait acknowledged in that person. The teacher can offer ideas to any students who are uncertain about what to write. Students deliver the letters — an excellent language arts activity.

A second way to handle this is for students to think of someone in their own lives, maybe an aunt or neighbor, and write the pleasing letters to them. This activity reinforces a positive socialization skill: that of appreciating others.

9. *Virtual or Real Interviews:* Interviewing another person can reinforce good socialization skills. Have students think of someone either in class or in the community — for example, school custodian, secretary, neighborhood grocer — and write at least five questions they will ask that person. They carry out the interviews and consolidate a report that can be either shared in groups or handed in. Help them think of open-ended, thought-promoting questions, such as: "What do you like best about . . .?" "What is your favorite . . .?" Remind students to avoid questions that require only a "yes" or "no" response.

10. *Practice Talk:* Many children and adults who have difficulty socializing well have specific difficulty when speaking to *some* people. This activity helps students understand that our approaches, vocabulary, and stances differ depending on whom we are speaking to. In language arts terms, this consciousness is referred to as pragmatics and its teaching is an important curriculum mandate. With the class, identify different categories of people that students talk to: peers, parents, seniors, dentists, teachers, principals, secretaries, custodians, retail clerks, police, grandparents, and so on. Discuss how we speak to various people in different roles in somewhat different ways; then, have groups of 3 or 4 create and present skits demonstrating how conversations on a single topic would differ. For instance, if the theme is asking for advice about a particular problem, one group talks with grandparents, one with the school secretary, one with a local police officer, and so on. Students will note that, although the basic premise is the same — namely, asking for help — in many cases, the manner of talking will differ. Performing and watching skits like these will provide students with confidence in future discussions with these people, thereby increasing their socialization skills.

Good Ideas

1. Have students pay attention to a television or online interview and note that interviewers avoid completely open-ended questions, such as "How did . . . make you feel?" Instead they provide a reaction and ask for qualification of it: "How angry did . . . make you feel?" This subtle interviewing technique helps to make an interview more interesting by suggesting reactions rather than putting the interviewee on the spot.

2. Interviews can be "virtual." Students can interview a virtual character, either real (e.g., a famous athlete) or fantasy (e.g., X-man). They create appropriate questions and devise possible responses. This activity works especially well if the class is studying historical characters they can research, pretend to interview, and provide the imagined-but-based-on-fact responses for as a report. Two students can work together and provide the report in Q and A format.

Good Reads

We Are Best Friends by Aliki
I Want to Play by Elizabeth Crary
That New Boy by Mary H. Lystad and Emily McCully
Fast Friends: Two Stories by James Stevenson
I Did It, I'm Sorry by Caralyn Buehner (illustrated by Mark Buehner)
Dude, That's Rude! (Get Some Manners) by Pamela Espeland and Elizabeth Verdick
What About Me? Twelve Ways to Get Your Parents' Attention (Without Hitting Your Sister) by Eileen Kennedy-Moore

Helping the Students Who *Really* Struggle with Socialization

Game playing and socialization activities are great, but some students still need teacher one-on-one intervention to help them with their socialization skills. Keep in mind that parental input is important, and that teachers and parents need to work together to help a child improve socializations skills. Parents can be encouraged to enroll their children in groups such as Boy Scouts, Girl Scouts, theatre groups, sports teams, and so on. These group activities naturally promote socialization in positive healthy environments. Just remind parents, if necessary, to maintain "balance" for their children.

The following Formula Five offers a one-on-one way for a teacher to work with a student with many socialization skills to master.

Meet in private.
Express concerns.
Invite responses.
Create an action plan.
Follow up.

Formula Five: Socializing the Un-socialized

Meet in private. Ask the student to meet with you at a specific time and place, for example, after school in the library, and preferably not at your desk. You want to avoid the "I'm in trouble" fear that is associated with meeting at the teacher's desk. Assure the student he is not in trouble, but that you have an idea you want to talk to him about.

Express concerns. Begin by thanking the student for coming; then, using "I" statements, express concern for his apparent socialization difficulties. Use kid-friendly language such as, "I'm a bit worried because I often see you alone in the playground and you don't look very happy about that," or "It concerns me that you seem to be getting into so many fights. You can't be happy if that's what's happening and I want you to feel better about . . ."

Invite responses. Once you have made your point, avoid belaboring it. Ask the student if he agrees with or understands what you have said. The answer will probably be "yes" or "no" so from there you can ask leading questions to gain more information. Continually paraphrase and summarize important points or thoughts as the two of you talk. Keep the discussion brief and to the point.

Create an action plan. Help the student come up with at least two ideas to try in the future. Never go into one of these situations without having some idea of what to suggest. Together, make a specific plan:

> Monday morning recess: Ask _____ to play catch.
> Afternoon recess: Smile at that person even if he is playing with someone else. Go to ____ and ask if he wants to play catch. If he doesn't, then . . .

Decide on a time to meet again to re-evaluate the plan. This time should be no longer than 3 or 4 days from the first meeting.

Follow up. Try to be visible for the student's first attempt at socialization both to give moral support as well as to pay attention to success or failure. Meet at the decided time and review the plan. If it worked, add to it. If it didn't work, try to figure out what went wrong and make changes.

The Bullying Dilemma

Bullying is any act that is deliberate, hurtful, frequently repeated, often insidious, and difficult to isolate. We are saturated by writing about it yet the problem still exists. I do not have the answer to the question on how to deal with it, but I can share some ideas that have worked *to some degree*. In today's schools, bullying is prevalent, and according to what teachers have told me, it is on the upsurge.

There are probably many reasons for the current upsurge, a few of which, I hope, will be of relevance to teachers in general. Bullies may be suffering from the sins of society; they may be victims of too much readily visible violence, which, in turn, comes with the frenzied expansion of technology. Many psychologists believe that witnessing violence leads to violent behavior. Teachers certainly have some control over this at least while children are at school. Another reason for the apparent increase in bullying may be that it is a silent reaction to home-based stresses and anxieties. Many parents today are suffering from, among other things, a failing economy, and this sort of anxiety cannot be hidden from children who, if lacking positive outlets for their own disquiet, resort to bullying. Finally, overwhelming curricula and higher-than-ever expectations for students to "learn everything" may be causing some children to rebel by bullying. No matter what the causes, however, bullying is a modern-school problem faced by modern-school teachers.

Since this is not a book focused *only* on bullying, the suggestions provided concentrate on covert bullying, the quietly disturbing interactions, the under-handed dealings where teachers know something untoward has happened but are not sure exactly what, and to whom, and by whom. Teachers constantly tell me these devious bully attacks cause them the most trouble. If a bully and his (or her) gang openly accost or verbally attack a child, the situation is obvious and intervention is usually possible. At the very least, some sort of behavior management is warranted and easily justified for the attackers.. However, when the bully is sneaky and the attacked child is frightened — too frightened to speak of the problem — the entire state of affairs can go unnoticed.

This type of bullying is called *relational aggression* by psychologists. It includes gossip, rumors, teasing, alienation, betrayal, humiliation, and censure, and in each case of it, someone usually suffers silently. Such aggression can come not only from peers but from adults. For instance, the adult who continually, unthinkingly, calls a child "stupid," "lazy," or "fat" is guilty of covert bullying.

What can teachers do?

First, they need to identify and define the problem. Although all children understand what a bully is, few are aware of all the covert actions that also consti-tute bullying. I recall a Grade 3 student, whom I'll call Janet, who was continually shaming another student, Amy, because she was overweight. When I asked Janet why she was bullying Amy, Janet looked surprised and said, "I'm not a bully. Bullies are mean and they beat you up. I'm not hitting her. I'm telling the *truth*!" That was when I realized how little students understand about bullying and that to deal with the situation, I needed to inform them. At that time in my career, though, I had no idea how to go about sharing what I knew in a way that would inform students without glamorizing bullying. After more than 30 years in the classroom, I have a much better grip on the situation. There really are positive steps teachers can take to establish an anti-bullying classroom climate. I suggest these steps be implemented early in the school year and reinforced continually thereafter.

Promoting zero tolerance for bullying

1. The teacher opens the subject by expressing verbally her zero tolerance for bullying. The class then discusses what constitutes bullying (all the covert tactics in addition to the physical) and a highly visible wall chart is posted. The teacher should include all the less visible bullying tactics, such as teasing, shaming, embarrassing, putting down, lying about, name-calling, being rude to, and not allowing involvement as well as any ideas the students can identify.

2. The teacher explains the consequences of any bullying activity. These easily carried out measures could include sending the bully home with a letter to parents or having the bully "do time" in the form of school–community work (e.g., emptying garbage). This response simulates the legal system. Often, bullies can relate to it more than being sent home, where they are usually able to justify their actions.

3. The teacher shares picture books about bullying. Good examples are *Oliver Button Is a Sissy* by Tomie dePaola, *5 Cheesy Stories: About Friendship, Bravery, Bullying and More* by Patsy Clairmont, and *The Berenstain Bears and the Bully* by Stan and Jan Berenstain. These serve as anticipatory sets for follow-up discussion about the topic. The more kids know about bullying, the less likely they are to become victims. When discussing bullying, I recommend using picture books even with older children and adolescents because often the illustrations are gripping and thought provoking. It's also good to read children's literature that includes ideas related to bullying — in particular, covert bullying, as in a foster child who is rejected openly by siblings — and invite discussions. Students can identify the bullying behaviors as well as the positive and perhaps negative ways they are handled.

4. The teacher keeps an eye out for changes in behavior in any of the students. There are, of course, many reasons for behavioral changes, but suspicion of bullying is certainly one. If this feeling of wariness exists, the teacher needs to be even more vigilant for a few days, documenting any, even subtle, changes in behavior. Although almost any change in behavior may suggest a child is the victim of covert bullying, these same changes can also point to many other problems. Caution is warranted. Possible symptoms of covert bullying include these:

- Child is withdrawn, depressed, more quiet than usual.
- Child's marks slip; appears disinterested in work.
- Child becomes clingy and tends to tattletale or whine.
- Child seems to develop almost hypochondriac tendencies, often finding physical reasons to avoid recess or outdoor activities.

These ideas pertaining to a zero tolerance policy on bullying constitute the ongoing considerations in the classroom. They are mainly preventive measures. As all teachers know, however, bullying will still exist and can be so insidious that seeing it and consequently dealing with it are difficult.

Keep in mind that in every instance of bullying, there are two casualties: the bully and the victim. It's easy to treat the victim, but the child who resorts to bullying behavior is suffering too. Effective teachers will want to help both parties. Remember that the child who least deserves love and positive attention needs it the most. I am not intending to undermine the suffering of the victim (this child needs immediate, concerned, and ongoing help), but rather to suggest that the

Whatever consequence(s) teachers establish, they must be cleared with the principal and a letter sent home early in the year notifying parents of the position taken. As a rule, this practice is a comfort to parents. Most schools have a zero tolerance policy for bullying.

teacher also try to find a way to deal with the bully. In so doing, the teacher may well prevent or at least lessen future bullying acts by this child.

Dealing with covert bullying

Most of us have at some time been guilty of covert bullying and certainly have suffered the consequences of it. That doesn't mean, however, that we should ignore it or allow our students to "tough it out." Adults who adopt the tough-it-out attitude often don't feel effective in dealing with the situation; they take this approach because they have no other. Concerned teachers, however, can take a stand, and when they do, children listen.

Often, children don't see themselves as bullies when they are "just teasing" or whispering. Once they understand that these behaviors reflect negatively upon them, many of the actions diminish or cease entirely. They all understand that a bully is "bad" or "wrong" — they just don't see themselves in that light. So, the teacher can use the following Formula Five.

Discuss.
Alter the point of view.
Write about it.
Role-play.
Isolate.

Formula Five: Dealing with Covert Bullying

Discuss. Conduct a class in which all aspects of bullying are shared (or reviewed), discussed openly, and even written about. Review the "bullying chart" from a previous lesson or create one now; then, have students define a bully, using as many of the descriptors as they want to. Be careful that students do not use specific names or accidentally point fingers.

Alter the point of view. Now, take an opposite approach and look at the situation from the bully's point of view. Doing so will seem strange to students until you point out that the bully is unhappy. There is a myth that bullies have low self-esteem. In fact, most of them are quite self-assured and receive a lot of attention for their behaviors; however, they aren't necessarily happy. The teacher should provide possible describing terms such as *cowardly, angry, anxious, hurt,* and *jealous*. By introducing the bully using these derogatory terms, there can be two possible outcomes: (1) Bullies view themselves differently and may work to lessen their adverse behaviors; (2) Victims see bullies differently and are less fearful. It is often useful to tell students that, in the long term, it is the bully one should feel sorry for: the bully doesn't know how to socialize properly and will eventually pay the price for negative behavior. This information doesn't lessen the pain experienced by the bullied, but it does give some power to them. Now they can choose to see the bully as a victim too, a victim of his or her own inadequacies. This approach is not intended to downplay the bullying behaviors; it is meant to give the bullied an additional tool for dealing with bullying. It tends to remove some of the fear experienced and replace it with a degree of control.

Write about it. Everyone has been bullied at some time or another and helping students understand this aids them in avoiding covert bullying especially. Encourage writing in a journal about how they felt when bullied. Assure them that no one will read these journals except you, and no evaluation will be given.

Role-play. Conduct a follow-up class on what to do if you are the victim of covert bullying. By giving students a concrete plan of action, teachers provide a weapon for self-defence. This action can be as simple as saying, "Stop it!" then turning deliberately away and leaving the situation, and telling someone, preferably a significant adult, what happened. There are three simple steps: (1) Stop, (2) Walk, and (3)

Tell. Sometimes, if potential bullies know that other children have been given tactics to deal with their teasing, humiliating, or mimicking behaviors, they will think twice before renewing such behaviors. Role-playing helps here. Break the class into groups of 3 to 5, and give each group a bully situation to act out with appropriate handling. Possible situations:

- You are walking home alone when you notice a girl in your class hanging out by the fence. She is there every day and when you walk past she calls you names. You keep walking and try not to react as the name-calling begins again.
- In the change room, you accidentally tear your shorts and another student starts laughing and humiliating you. This student and her pals seem to jeer at every little thing you do or say, and now they are laughing at your clothes too.
- Every day at lunch break, you have to walk past a group of students who appear to be whispering about you and snickering to themselves.
- You are required to work with a partner in Science class, and your partner keeps calling you "stupid" and "dummy" when you make mistakes.
- When teams are picked in Physical Education, you are always picked last, and the others say things like "I guess I have to take her" or "Great! I'm stuck with her!"

Isolate. Negative behavior is so ingrained in some bullies that it is difficult to help them, but teachers are morally obliged to try. A few facts about bullies are worth reviewing. They are often

- attention seeking
- poor at socializing
- followed by a "gang" that reinforces the behavior
- deluded about their popularity when, in fact, most students are afraid of them
- quick to pick up on the victims who "don't tell" and the teachers who fail to react
- excited by their deviant behavior
- in denial as to the injustice of their actions — "It was her fault because she . . ."

When a bully is not easily convinced to change the behavior, it is necessary for the teacher to isolate him and follow a set of steps.

1. Ask the bully why he has been isolated.
2. Offer a concise explanation if the response is not given accurately.
3. Avoid any mention of the shortcomings of the bully: "You do not know how to socialize . . ." Deal with what has happened only.
4. Have the bully write a letter home explaining what has happened. Stay with the offender during the letter writing, and make sure that the letter doesn't "blame" or make excuses.
5. Mail the letter to the home. Doing this not only ensures that it gets there but also shows the offender how important it is.
6. Follow up with a call home in about a week (give the letter time to arrive). Simply say you are following up on the letter (just in case the document got "waylaid" from the mailbox) and are available if the parent(s) want to talk with you.
7. If parents can come for a discussion, be sure to have some options available for them (e.g., a course on pro-social behavior, a checklist of good socialization skills, the phone number of a group such as Big Brothers Big Sisters, or the name of a counselor or school psychologist).
8. In the classroom, you may wish to have the offender sign a contract indicating an intention to change behaviors and keep a personal record that will log

Bursting Bad Balloons

Here is a way for children to get rid of negative thoughts. Have them close their eyes and imagine they each have a big "bad" balloon in their hands. They blow up their balloons and with each breath, they push "bad" or "negative" thoughts into the balloons along with the air. If angry at someone or something, they put the anger in the balloon by formulating the anger into words in their minds. *"I'm really mad at Chris because he. . . ."* They can keep repeating the same thought or add to it: *"I feel like punching him."* They keep on with this until their balloons are full; then, they tie them and let them go. They imagine the balloons flying away as if filled with helium; then, they shoot an arrow or dart at them and pop them. When the balloons break, all the bad thoughts are exploded and disappear — this simple imagery works amazingly well for most children. Later, if you sense a child is angry or frustrated, simply invite him to blow up another bad balloon.

good social interactions. Avoid having the offender record bullying behaviors as doing so would tend to reinforce the behavior(s) you are trying to diminish. Reinforce the positive only.

Good Reads

Wendy and the Bullies by N. K. Robinson
Oliver Button Is a Sissy: Overcoming Bullying by Tomie dePaola
The Bully: A Discussion and Activity Story by Rita Y. Toews
Why Is Everybody Always Picking on Me? A Guide to Understanding Bullies for Young People by Terrence Webster-Doyle
Arthur's April Fool by Marc Brown
Blubber by Judy Blume (a chapter book)

Independence of Self

Personal independence is all tied together with awareness of self and the ability to socialize well. Why then, is it a separate section in *Teaching in Troubled Times*? Today's teachers constantly tell me about a growing lack of independence in their students and frequently ask how they can develop independence in both elementary schoolchildren and adolescents.

It is possible to suggest reasons for the growing lack of independence in children, perhaps the most common point being the direct result of a frightening society where parents worry all the time about their children's safety. Gone are the days of children playing in parks until dark, running freely along creek banks, riding bicycles through forest trails, and so on. Our world today is deemed too unsafe for such reckless ventures, so children are kept at home, often glued to televisions or video games. Parents are doing their best to protect their offspring in a society that seems filled with predators, temptations, and evils lurking everywhere. One psychologist even said that childhood today was more like a jail sentence than a time of joyful freedom. There is an unfortunate element of truth in those words. We keep our children safe by keeping them under lock and key, by driving them everywhere, by picking them up even if they are only a couple of blocks from home, by cautioning them about the potential horrors "out there," by insisting they carry cell phones everywhere, by, as one mother put it, "making the kids into wimps." I'm not sure if that is true, but I do know that many children today are considerably less independent than they were 20 or even 10 years ago.

The reasons for this lack of student independence are unimportant — what teachers can do to remedy the situation is vital. The following list summarizes well-known and well-used teacher techniques. It is included here as a reminder and re-focuser for educators. Because teachers will already be familiar with these concepts, only a brief description is provided together with an indication as to how each fosters student independence.

Ten ways to foster independence in the classroom

1. **Give clear directions.** Provide slow, clear oral directions together with written when possible, and be sure students can repeat them back to you before allowing them to begin. Doing so fosters independence by allowing students to begin work on their own without prompting, thus helping them to feel

1. Give clear directions.
2. Set clear boundaries
3. Accept and use failure constructively.
4. Maintain consistent consequences.
5. Provide choices and responsibilities.
6. Teach social skills.
7. Teach problem solving.
8. Provide for success situations.
9. Model independence.
10. Respect students.

Use the words "your choice" and "your responsibility" often in the class, and students will become familiar with them and their meanings.

Good Idea

On your desk, keep a Success journal, where you list all the names of students in your class on a graph-type paper that will allow you to quickly check boxes adjacent to names as individuals have little successes. A quick check at the end of the day will show who might need a success situation soon.

self-confident. (Avoid the temptation to repeat directions many times as this is counterproductive to fostering independence.)

2. **Set clear boundaries.** Clearly inform students of boundaries, such as time limits, location boundaries such as "in these areas only," and limits of acceptable error. This practice fosters independence by showing students the areas within which they can *choose* success and cooperation. Any element of choice encourages self-sufficiency.

3. **Accept and use failure.** Discuss failure as an opportunity for improvement and insist students independently find ways to use their failures in that way. You thereby foster independence by encouraging students to grow from their mistakes and appreciate how this can be a lifelong learning style.

4. **Maintain consistent consequences.** Once consequences have been established and shared, ensure that they are consistently enforced. Doing so fosters independence by allowing students to know exactly what the repercussions of their actions, whether positive or negative, will be, thereby giving them the *choice* to behave in a certain manner or accept those consequences.

5. **Provide choices and responsibilities.** I have already mentioned the importance of "choice" as a promoter of independence, and teachers can deliberately work choices into daily classroom settings: "Do either . . . or . . . You choose." Similarly, providing as many responsibilities as possible, together with the reasons for those responsibilities, is helpful: "It is your responsibility to keep your desk tidy because . . ."

6. **Teach social skills.** This topic was covered under "Top 10 Class Activities That Promote Socialization" on pages 56–60. Suffice to say that teaching social skills fosters independence by helping students find success in socialization, which bolsters their self-confidence.

7. **Teach problem solving.** This area of independence is huge, so huge, in fact, that I recently wrote an entire book about it, *Desperately Seeking Solutions*. Teachers need to be alert to situations where they can allow students to solve their own problems, both large and small, and to integrate problem-solving skills into daily curriculum. Problem solving fosters independence by giving students confidence and personal power.

8. **Provide for success situations.** Teachers are aware of the importance of success for student growth. This point serves as a little reminder that all students need to experience success regularly; it is essential to find ways for each student to be successful at *something*, even throwing a ball, taking messages to the office, or cleaning up the reading corner. Doing so fosters independence by pumping up students' self-confidence, a true sign of independence.

9. **Model independence.** Remember that the teacher, in students' eyes, is a paragon of, well, just about everything, so what you model they will emulate. Take every opportunity to model independent thinking and behavior, and talk about it when appropriate. For example, mention how you changed a tire on your car, fixed the copier machine, or made some important decision to do something difficult for you. Such behavior fosters independence by activating the I-see-I-do frame of thought.

Instant Memory Motivator

The ability to recall facts, faces, and so on is an important part of becoming independent. Once you have discussed this idea and provided examples, such as not having to phone home to ask where a pen is, invite the students to play Instant Memory, possibly in pairs. Show them one of the following selections:

- Objects on overhead: Show paper clip, scissors, pen . . . about 20 items.
- Large picture with many details: Students recall details, such as how many children, how dressed, and so on.
- Designs, such as a kaleidoscope: Students look, then attempt to copy from memory.
- A piece of writing, perhaps a portion of a story or essay, shown on overhead: Children in Grades 5 and up view, attempt to memorize, and then reproduce accurately.

Students study the display for 60 seconds, you remove or cover it, and then students try to recall the details.

Respect Day

Maybe once a month, have a Respect Day during which you encourage students to express in words what they respect in others. For example, one student might tell another that she respects his ability to work quietly while the class is noisy.

A good way to start this off is with a short brainstorming session about traits that students might respect in others. They can draw on this list later on. Follow this with a "think time" of 5 to 10 minutes, where students can talk quietly with a peer to share and discuss possible ideas.

At the end of the day, you may want to give every student a note telling one thing you respect him or her for.

10. **Respect your students.** Sometimes we are so concerned about the futures of our students we forget that they are real people right now, today. Remember that anything that would cause you pain or hurt will likely cause double the pain or hurt in a child. Always try to see your students with open eyes and open hearts. Doing so fosters independence by improving self-confidence and feelings of self-worth, which, in turn, serve to empower the students to be more independent.

Good Reads

Serendipity by Stephen Cosgrove (illustrated by Robin James) (Serendipity Books)
The Art Lesson by Tomie dePaola
Judy Moody Declares Independence by Megan McDonald and Peter H. Reynolds (a chapter book)
Ella Sarah Gets Dressed by Margaret Chodos-Irvine
A Bad Case of Stripes by David Shannon

Wellness of Self

Wellness covers a range of concepts including all areas related to mental and physical health that result in an overall feeling of self-satisfaction and happiness. Teachers are naturally concerned with the wellness of their students and have at least some degree of control over its components.

A focus on wellness is relatively new. Particularly current are the concerns with childhood obesity and physical fitness. These are addressed in this chapter.

Wellness — Matters of Weight

It appears that far too many youngsters are overweight today. Statistics Canada states that "obesity rates in children have almost tripled in the last 25 years. Approximately 26% of Canadian children ages 2–17 years old are currently overweight or obese." Reasons are many, and in most cases, teachers have little control over them. Situations such as the fear-based reluctance to allow children to play outside after school — thereby getting vigorous exercise; the number of families where both parents have to work long hours to meet financial needs, thereby losing considerable control over what children eat; the ready availability of fast foods and junk foods; and, of course, the fixation with video and computer games as opposed to team sports or athletic ventures may all help to create overweight children. And unfortunately, these children may end up with not only low self-esteem and depression, but with Type II diabetes, increased risk of high blood pressure, bone and joint problems, sleep disorders, cardiovascular disease, and potentially fatal health problems as adults.

Typically, children who are overweight or obese have extremely negative self-images. They are teased. School years are a crisis time for development of self-confidence, and these children often feel isolated, different, unhappy, even depressed, with resulting low confidence and, too often, poor work habits and scholastic achievement. As noted previously, there are more and more of these children in today's classrooms, and teachers will want to help them become healthier while developing a more positive sense of self.

Demonstrating unconditional acceptance

Teachers try to be fair, to treat all students equally, but they are human and sometimes this is difficult. However, if they are to help students develop positive self-concepts, it is important for them to show genuine unconditional acceptance of all and to endorse discussions, thoughts, and actions that promote unconditional acceptance of peers. Here are some of the ways.

- **Model acceptance.** Accept and value all children's ideas, work, feelings, and thoughts. Be aware that it can be easy to veer towards the good students, the attractive students, the better adjusted students, and to unconsciously overlook the overweight ones. This is not a teaching flaw; it is a fact of nature and you simply need to be aware of it in order to overcome it. Make it a point to obviously accept and value those low self-image overweight students.
- **Provide alternative images.** Most images of adults and children in readers, on television, on posters, and in movies are of the slender, sometimes anorexic looking models. Young Hollywood stars, for example, are notorious for being far too thin to be healthy, but these are the images students want to emulate. It is helpful if you can find images of more "normal," even chubby characters who are successful and likeable, and point out their uniqueness.

  By constantly reminding children that each person is unique and that you do not condone the too skinny appearance of models, for example, you are lending credence to alternative images and are accepting children for who they are, not what they look like. Some companies, including Dove, are beginning to use almost chubby models. A bit of searching online or in books and magazines will probably result in finding some images of happy, healthy, productive "chubby kids." The idea is not to condone being obese, but to help children find a sense of connectedness with others while working to improve their personal health.
- **Squelch stereotypes.** Naturally, as a model and teacher you will take this approach with all stereotypes, but sometimes the biases about overweight children go unseen except by the children themselves (e.g., the chubby child not picked for a team because it's assumed she can't run quickly when, in fact, she

Good Idea

Challenge students to research other cultures in which being overweight has been considered positive. For example, in Mauritania, a country in western Africa, obesity is celebrated among females, and girls are force-fed to increase their overall weight. In Nigeria many tribes encourage both men and women to "fatten up" before marriage as a symbol of beauty. Some tribes such as the Hottentot, natives of southwestern Africa closely related to the Bushmen, still gauge female beauty by their bulk and, in particular, by the amount of fat around their middles.

runs well). Being vigilant and stopping these stereotypes as soon as they begin or even before is a teacher's professional obligation. René Descartes wrote: "The chief cause of human errors is to be found in the prejudices picked up in childhood." Include activities that will show off the skills and aptitudes of the overweight student(s), perhaps creative or dramatic endeavors.

Strategies for correcting misconceptions about weight

- *The Role of Heredity:* It has been proven that genes play a part in the predisposition towards obesity. Some people simply do not process foods the same way as others. By discussing this in class, you can help reduce some of the anxiety felt by overweight students. It is important not to provide an excuse, however, for the condition, but to let children know that while not entirely at fault, they can still have control over their own situations.
- *Think-Aloud:* A strategy that I have witnessed working well is the teacher using a think-aloud approach while watching a movie, television clip, or DVD, or even viewing pictures in a book. For example, if while watching a film with the class, you notice that one actor is extremely thin, you might stop the movie for a moment and say, "She sure is skinny — I don't like that look." By expressing your dislike of the too thin look, you are indirectly lending support to the overweight students.

  The next step is to provide students with magazine pictures of people with a variety of body types and have them in pairs or groups of 3 or 4 use the think-aloud approach when examining the pictures. Mingle with the groups and listen carefully for negative comments that you can gently alter. For example, "That man is fat" can be changed to "That man is heavy." At the same time, reinforce positive statements.
- *Toy Talk:* Some children's toys promote the image of a skinny body. Consider Barbie and Ken dolls. Their measurements, if transposed according to scale to a real person, would look not only ridiculous but freakish. Yet these toys are hugely popular with young girls. If possible, bring a couple of these toys to class and discuss them with the students, leading the talk to how ridiculous the body shapes are.

Promoting good nutrition

Although pinpointing specific causes of childhood obesity is impossible, it is possible to provide teachers with suggestions for dealing with it in their classrooms. These classroom strategies benefit all students; they teach about being healthy and happy and accepting of others, so are valuable lessons. They are probably familiar to most teachers, but reinforcement of common ideas is always useful.

1. Be a good model: Bring only nutritious snacks (e.g., an apple) to school yourself, and leave it conspicuously on your desk.
2. Offer specific verbal reinforcement for good snacks you see in your classroom. "I'm glad to see you brought an apple for recess because it helps to clean your teeth."
3. Start a "Snack trade" program, whereby you prepare a number of small, healthy snacks, such as dried fruits, nuts, or raisins, tied in squares of plastic or dollar-store baggies. These are kept in the classroom and if a child brings a non-nutritious snack (e.g., a chocolate bar), the teacher can offer to trade for one of the nutritious ones. Keep in mind that some kids don't have a chance to bring a healthy snack — the trade program remedies this without

Good Ideas

1. Invite students to take the measurements of a Barbie doll, and work out what they would look like on a person of their height. This activity could be done as a class. The results are quite humorous.
2. Challenge students to find examples of toys that show both healthy and unhealthy bodies, and bring their findings to a class discussion. For example, a good old teddy bear may be rotund, but much loved.

Sometimes, just bringing these ideas to the students' attention can provide a huge boost to confidence.

causing embarrassment (and the chocolate will quickly disappear if left in the teachers' lounge). This program doesn't have to be expensive, and most schools have a flexible budget that could help. If not, a fund raiser for the program would most likely be supported by parents and school.

4. If you feel comfortable disclosing personal information, and have had, or know someone who has had, difficulty losing weight, sharing this with students, together with some of the problems associated with your "personal" overweight condition, can be helpful. Remember that students view you as the knowledgeable leader and will relate to what you say, making their own difficulties seem less frightening. "Teacher was like me and she . . ."

5. Institute Healthy Snack journals. Have students keep a record of healthy snacks consumed during the week. They can hand in the journal on Fridays and you can write a positive comment.

Teaching the fast-food traps

Teachers have little control over the ready availability of fast foods, and parents, swamped with work and responsibilities, cannot be faulted for being tempted by the inexpensive and quick availability of fast foods. Unfortunately, children are drawn to these foods as well, and the best educators can hope to do is *teach the traps*, as outlined in the following Formula Five: Fast Food Foibles. (Do remember to point out that most fast-food restaurants now offer healthier choices as well as the regular fare.)

This Formula Five is good to share with students, mount in brief form on a wall, and refer to often. You may want to begin by defining "foibles," which are minor weaknesses. In this case, explain that you are considering fixations on junk foods as minor weaknesses because students have the power within themselves to overcome any such weaknesses. Point out that this Formula Five is an acrostic spelling "demon." Fast foods can be viewed as demons. You might also note the merits of alliteration — Fast Food Foibles — as a memory-aiding device.

Dubious portions.
Empty calories.
Money thieves.
Overfatty.
Nothing special calories.

Formula Five: Fast Food Foibles

Dubious portions. The whole idea of portion control needs to be discussed with children who tend to overeat something they enjoy, such as certain fast foods. Ask questions such as these:

- How much food is enough?
- How do you know when you're full?
- Do some foods make you feel full faster?
- What happens when you overeat?

Empty calories. Teaching students about the difference between empty calories and healthy calories doesn't take long and the information provides them with a lifelong learning plan for good nutrition. The relatively new term *empty calories* describes foods high in calories but low in nutritional values — that is, most fast foods and junk foods. Show students a couple of examples of foods containing healthy calories — an apple, a handful of nuts, a cereal bar (check the sugar content) — as well as some items containing empty calories — a small candy bar, a small bag of candies, a can of soda. Point out that the healthy calorie foods provide more lasting energy than the empty calorie ones and invite discussion about this.

Encourage children to read labels on products and check for calories, sugars, and so on.

Money thieves. "But it only cost me a dollar," the chubby lad said of his second burger of the day. What children may fail to realize is how quickly the "dollars" accumulate. A Grade 7 student who ate fast food every day for lunch was challenged to keep a record of how much he spent and was unpleasantly surprised at the results. Invite students to think of alternatives for the money spent on fast foods. When the boy in the previous anecdote switched from fast foods to healthy salmon sandwiches he made every morning, he saved enough money in a few months to purchase a jacket he had had his eye on.

Overfatty. Most children today are aware of the pitfalls of fatty foods but may not be aware of the high fat content of their favorite fast food. Finding this out by researching the various fast-food chains and their most popular items can be an eye-opening experience.

Nothing special calories. Fast foods are notorious for providing that slow, sloth-like feeling as opposed to the energy children need. Remind them that a meal should give them energy, not take it. Return to the concept of empty calories and the discussion about which foods provide healthy calories; those are the ones that provide the most energy also. (Remember that athletes ingest meals high in carbohydrates prior to strenuous activity; you might discuss this with students, especially if they are already familiar with the idea.)

Food Court Trial

This activity involves students in small groups of 3 or 4 researching a favorite fast food, perhaps fries, potato chips, or soda, and then creating skits court-and-jury style in which the chosen fast food is brought to trial. Food Court Trial is highly motivating to students and the inherent learning is excellent. The excerpt below provides information as to how the activity is played out.

Food Court Trial: Example

JUDGE: Court is in order. Soda, please stand and state your case.

SODA: I have been unfairly accused. I'm sweet and lovely and I quench thirst and . . .

SODA'S DEFENCE LAWYER: . . . and poor Soda here is accused of being harmful to health. Not true, I say.

JUDGE: What do you have to say, Mr. Prosecutor?

PROSECUTOR: Soda is filled with salt, and we all know how harmful salt is to the body.

DEFENCE: Where does it say on Soda's label that he has salt?

PROSECUTOR: Two hundred milligrams of sodium. Right here. (*points to label*)

SODA: (*jumping up*) OK, but what about taste? I'm so sweet!

PROSECUTOR: Sugar! Look at all the sugar. Sugary, salty water — that's what you are.

DEFENCE: But he's so tasty, orange, lemon, grape . . .

PROSECUTOR: All artificial flavors — no health benefits at all.

DEFENCE: Thirst quencher. He quenches thirst.

PROSECUTOR: Actually, it's been proven that drinking soda makes you thirstier . . .

Finding the Hidden Fat

Some children think fat content is high only if a food is deep fried. A quick lesson on hidden fat content in favorite foods (e.g., chocolate bars) can be informative and helpful. Encourage the reading of labels and provide information about the negative effects of eating too much fat. I don't think you need to talk about kinds of fats. Mostly you are drawing attention to fatty foods in general.

Good Idea

This activity makes an excellent concert presentation where a number of poor food choices are presented in a courtroom and told to support their positions. It also works well for an Open House. Groups can be stationed around the school, presenting their food court trials.

SODA: I object!
JUDGE: Sit down, Soda.

Once the skit has concluded, students would identify all the less than admirable qualities of a soda drink.

Helping overweight students directly

Sometimes, you may want to sit together with an overweight child who is struggling with poor self-esteem and work out a plan of action. Of course, parents should be contacted; you should ask permission to attempt an at-school intervention. Most parents will give permission. Assuming this is the case, there are a few strategies you can employ, starting with a sincere discussion with the student in which concerns are voiced. Remember that the student will likely be defensive about his weight and may initially reject help, but if you are persistent, caring, and supportive, eventually most children will accept help. The following list is provided in the sequence with which ideas are best used.

1. *Initial Discussion:* Explain your concern for the child, using "I" statements: "I sense that you are unhappy with the way you look. I want to help and I have some ideas." Invite him to talk about his feelings. Indicate that you accept, understand, and appreciate him as an individual.

2. *Snack Attack:* Many overweight kids eat poor snacks; this is a good place to start. If you have initiated a "Snack trade" program (see page 70), reinforce it. If you are not using this strategy, it may be worthwhile to create a plan between the two of you whereby the student privately shares the day's snacks with you each morning, and together you assess for content and make a trade, if necessary. You will have to have some healthy snacks on hand.

3. *Food Journal:* Provide the student with a small journal, maybe a daily agenda book from a dollar store, and show her how to record everything eaten each day. At the end of a set time (e.g., a week), go over the food choices with the student and make positive suggestions. Just keeping an accurate record of everything consumed creates a food awareness that helps many people lose weight. You will have no control over the accuracy of the entries, but show respect and accept them, even if you doubt their truthfulness.

4. *Follow-up Meetings:* Each time you get together to discuss the situation, set the time for a follow-up meeting. Doing this is important for two reasons. The student needs to know you care enough to keep meeting and also needs the control that comes from having to report to you regularly. Be sure to reinforce effort as well as successes.

Wellness — Fit for Life

In today's world we are inundated with fitness facts, fitness ideas, and lack of fitness warnings. As a teacher, you will understand the importance of physical activity in students, but given the extent of current curricula, finding time for fitness beyond the required physical education program is often difficult to do.

Food Journal Favor

I helped an overweight Grade 7 student begin a Food Journal. After three weeks she hadn't lost any weight, even though she should have according to what she said she had been eating. She decided to stop the journal and I respected her wishes. It had been almost the end of the school year.

During the summer, the girl's family moved, and it was not until a couple of years later, she showed up in my classroom after school. She looked healthy and svelte. She confided that she had "cheated" in the Food Journal but had felt terribly guilty about it. During that summer, every time she went to eat something "with empty calories," she was aware of it and didn't eat it.

"Guilt made me lose weight," she joked.

I knew it was the Food Journal that had helped — eventually.

Thousands of fitness ideas are available online, in magazines and books, and from peers, but busy teachers don't have time to search them out. Consequently, I have included quick, in-class activities that help boost overall fitness and suggest to the students your own commitment to being fit and healthy. These activities take little time, can be carried out at or beside desks, and can even work to refocus or motivate students who are lethargic, restless, or disinterested. They are great early morning or late afternoon wakeups. They constitute "Fitness at your Fingertips."

One thing to keep in mind, however, is that you are a model — in this case, a fitness model — so, if at all possible, do the activities with the students.

Fitness at your fingertips

Muscles: Shoulders (deltoids), thighs (quadriceps), knee and shoulder joints

- *Action Patterns:* Ask students to stand beside desks with both arms elevated as high as possible. Choose a "magic number" (any number from 1 to 5). Count from 1 to 5 repeatedly and every time you come to the magic number, students must lift a knee and pull arms down, then rapidly return to the hand-raised position. To make it more difficult, you can say the numbers randomly rather than in sequence, or change the activity — jump, touch your toes, turn around. This activity is more difficult than it sounds.

Muscles: Arms and shoulders plus whole body

- *Wind-Me-Up:* Students work with partners. *A* is a toy; *B* is a toy owner. The owner must mime winding the toy, using big circular movements behind it. (The winding involves full arm and shoulder range of motion, an important fitness attribute.) The toy then moves randomly (in place or around the room) until the teacher cues that the "wind" is dying down, at which time the toy slows down until it stops. Partners change places.

Muscles: Hands and fingers, wrist joints

- *Thermometer Hands:* Sitting or standing, students flick fingers and wrists as if "shaking down a thermometer." Don't allow this to continue for more than about 30 seconds as it can become painful if overdone — if done correctly, it is a great exercise for hands. Tell students to "feel the blood making your hands tingle" once they stop. This sensation can be equated to the way any physical exercise rushes extra blood to limbs — a good thing!

Muscles: Arms, hands, wrist joints

- *Doorknobs:* Students stand and hold arms away from their bodies, parallel to the floor. While holding them thus, they mime turning doorknobs with both hands. As they "turn" (using hands only — no arm involvement other than the small movements of the forearm that happen naturally), you as teacher continually change the sizes of the doorknobs: "The knob is getting smaller, the size of an egg, now bigger, the size of a cantaloupe." Time the activity, stopping after 60 seconds the first time, but gradually increasing the duration for future times. This activity is naturally tiring.

Muscles: Arms, shoulders, back, elbow and shoulder joints

- *Hummingbirds:* Students stand beside desks; on cue, they mime being hummingbirds with rapid wing movements. Students can move their wings on the spot or around the room. You may wish to first remind students of the speed with which these birds move and yet appear so delicate and controlled.

Muscles: Biceps and triceps (arms), forearms, hands, wrist and finger joints

- *Drummers:* Sitting at their desks, students imagine the desk tops to be drums. On cue, they begin drumming, using pencils, rulers, or fingers. You may wish to lead them with a specific beat or pattern that keeps changing, or you may just allow free drumming for about two minutes. This exercise permits a great discharge of energy as well as being an arm-and-shoulder workout.

Muscles: Full legs, hip joints, knees, and ankle joints

- *Artistic Toes:* Sitting at desks, students lift a leg and point the toe, then draw in the air some object suggested by you or a student (e.g., a rabbit, a happy face, a wagon, a car). You can increase the difficulty by having the drawn item "come to life" and start moving — the rabbit hops, the car rolls. Another alternative is to have children work in pairs and together, using a foot each, they draw. Be sure to have them draw with both legs. Artistic Toes is an excellent leg and foot exercise, especially since the toes must remain pointed. (How can you paint or draw with the whole foot?) One additional alternative is to work with a partner and have one member guess what the other is drawing with toes.

Muscles: Full body involvement

- *Quick Sixty:* Standing beside desks, students either run or march quickly on the spot for 60 seconds. Or, they can alter running and marching on teacher cues. The time can be gradually extended. This activity promotes aerobic capacity and often energizes lethargic students. A good rule to provide and reinforce is "silent movement," which inhibits noisy feet-thumping and hence, potentially joint-injuring, jarring movements.

Muscles: Full body involvement with focus on legs and knees

- *Stair Climbing:* Climbing real stairs is the best way to handle this activity, but many schools today do not have stairs, so we simulate stair climbing. (Of course, if you do have access to stairs, use them if possible.) To simulate stair climbing, have students pretend to ascend slowly, lifting knees as high as possible and counting the steps (about 20 is good). When they reach the top, they stretch high then touch their toes before descending quickly, taking smaller steps as if running downhill. Repeat several times.

Muscles: Full body

Tell students *not to drop their heads backwards.* Neck circles move through the front and sides, but rather than back or behind, the head simply moves to the side, which protects the integrity of the neck.

- *Circling:* Standing beside desks, students circle each body part in both directions. Begin by holding arms loosely and circling wrists, then elbows, then shoulders. Move to necks. Move to trunk circles and then follow with feet, knees, and hips. The final circles are "whole bodies." Leave this as an open invitation and let students interpret how to "circle your whole body." There is no right or wrong way to do this, so encourage creativity. This activity takes joints through a whole range of motion, an important fitness pursuit.

Muscles: Focus on thighs (quadriceps) and hamstrings, plus knee joints and supporting tissues

- *Duck Walk:* Students squat down with hands on thighs and "waddle" around trying to keep their bodies as close to the floor as possible, like ducks.

Muscles: Feet, calves, and legs; some back involvement

- *Heel-toe Cat Walk:* Tell students this is a very quiet movement (like cats on the prowl). First, they walk on tiptoes, then on teacher's cue, switch to walking on heels. Keep changing them from toes to heels at regular intervals.

Muscles: Legs and body core (abdominals and back)

- *Seated Cyclists:* Tell students to sit sideways at their desks or on chairs moved away from tables, with about a hand span between back and chairback. Then, holding both sides of their seats, they lean back (to about 45 degrees), and pedal both legs as if riding a bike.

- *The Final Stretch:* Stretching is often overlooked. At the beginning of the day, take up to five minutes to teach students to stretch properly. By so doing, you will be giving them both an important life tool and a way to promote alertness of mind and body for the first class. The following stretches are all done in or beside the desk. They are listed in what I consider to be the best order: the most important stretches first. Each stretch is held for 15 seconds.

1. Stand/sit as tall as possible. Reaching for the sky, clasp hands above head and arch back; then, alternately pull the arms over the head, holding each pull for 15 seconds. (Left hand pulls right arm by grabbing right wrist and pulling towards the left.)
2. Stand/sit tall then lean over to the floor and hang (like a monkey).
3. Stand beside desk and put heel on the desk seat. Keep the leg (on the seat) straight and lean towards it as far as possible.

4. Stand/sit with back straight, lean alternately to the right (do not lean forward), letting right arm drop to the right as left arm reaches over the head. Hold and then alternate sides.
5. Sit/stand and rotate trunk by reaching with both hands as far to the left as possible then making a big circle (washing a table top) with arms. Reverse directions. No holding here but encourage full trunk flexion and extension.
6. Sit and hold the back of the chair by reaching arms behind while leaning forward until arms are fully extended.

Promoting appreciation of fitness and physical activity

Teacher-as-fitness-model must be emphasized. You don't have to be a weight lifter or even a fitness buff to model fitness for your students. You can talk about it, even to the point where you self-disclose that you would like to be more fit, and most certainly you can reinforce physical activity you see in your students.

The following are a few ideas for in-class daily promotion of fitness. The goal is to get students thinking of fitness as a lifelong activity for overall health and wellness.

- **Display fitness or physical activity posters.** Ask students to obtain as many fitness pictures or posters as possible and help create the display.
- **Invite fitness gurus to visit the class and talk to students.** By gurus, I mean anyone with an interest in and some knowledge of fitness. Ask at any local gym or club; trainers or instructors are usually very willing to provide this free service. Before someone comes, have students create good questions to ask.
- **Prompt students to keep Fitness Logs.** Recording everything they do that is considered a physical activity (e.g., walking to school; using stairs instead of elevators) often helps promote physical activities. A good follow-up is the creation of a collage or poster illustrating all the fitness activities a student has taken part in over a set time.
- **Create "Instead of" charts.** In small groups have students make charts that indicate what they could do "instead of" something that does not promote fitness. Example:

Instead of	Fitness Choice
watching TV	ride my bike
sitting on the swing	climb the monkey bar
getting a ride to school	walk with a friend

Teachers may find it helpful to keep in mind an insight from the Shakyamuni Buddha. The Buddha stated that the mind is everything — what you think you become. Teachers need to consider this because they have so much control over the minds, and hence the lives, of their students. They can do much to empower their students to be self-aware, self-confident, well socialized, independent, conscious of good nutrition and physical fitness, and consequently, generally happy and productive individuals. They can lead their students to the "I think I can" state of mind where, in keeping with the Buddha's insight, they become better people because they think they can.

CHAPTER 4

Concerning Parents Today

"When you put faith, hope, and love together, you [parents] can raise positive kids in a negative world."

— Zig Ziglar

Parents are one of a teacher's greatest resources. In the words of Peter Ustinov, "parents are the bones on which children cut their teeth," and all our students are in possession of a full set of teeth when they reach our classrooms. Consequently, teachers need to involve parents, understand parents' concerns, and accept parents' rules, expectations, and limitations. I recall a teacher, a new parent herself, saying in wonderment, "I never really understood parents' unconditional love and rose-colored glasses where their kids were concerned until now." Being a parent *does* help to understand parenting, but not all teachers have this opportunity; even those who do often need a little guidance in order to work effectively with the parents of their students.

Teachers must realize how much parents tend to worry about their children. Parents worry about the safety of their children not only when they travel to and from school, but also while at school. They worry about unfamiliarity with what their children are learning or should be learning at school, and what they are learning or shouldn't be learning outside of school. They worry about giving too much or too little support and assistance. They worry that the teachers might not be good enough, strict enough, gentle enough, knowledgeable enough, or approachable enough, and that the school might not be the best learning environment for their children. True, many of these trepidations have always plagued parents, but the troubles related to living in today's world seem to have heightened parental apprehension.

Without a doubt, parenting is tough. Parents, aware that most children cite them as their primary role models, uneasily wonder how well they serve as exemplary models. They may be confused by conflicting views on home schooling versus private schooling versus public schooling, on how much is *too* much when providing children with products, support, controls, discipline, and even affection. Today's parents, frequently entangled in financial insecurity, overwork, and uncertainty, may struggle with both their personal and parenting roles.

It behooves teachers, therefore, not only to be aware of the concerns parents own, but also to be prepared to offer support and assistance when possible. Parents, like students, view teachers as authority figures, as professionals who have answers, and people who are there to help. In other words, they view teachers accurately. The goal of this chapter of *Teaching in Troubled Times* is to provide teachers with some answers for parents. Teaching is a dynamic process. Teachers are constantly reassessing what is important for the success of their students; it may well be that allaying some parents' fears may be integral to that success. Just as parents are an important resource for teachers, so should teachers be an important resource for parents.

The areas identified for this chapter include family dynamics, tough topics, and safety first.

Modern Family Dynamics

In today's troubled times, family dynamics have changed, and some of them may present difficulties for children. When these difficulties are expressed during the school day, they become the teacher's responsibility. There may be, for example, an unbalanced emphasis on material success at home that interferes with practical child views of the world. Or there may be expectations for academic achievement that cause unhealthy child self-concepts if attaining the goals is impossible. In addition, the modern world is said to be experiencing family failings. Whether true or not, it is true that teachers seem to have more of the responsibilities of child rearing, while being prohibited from having rights to discipline. John Sculley said, "We expect teachers to handle teenage pregnancy, substance abuse, and the failings of the family. Then we expect them to educate our children." Somehow, teachers have to know how to work effectively with whatever manner of family or lack of family their students come from, and also to maintain professionalism under a strict code of what they can and cannot do.

It is not within the boundaries of this book to discuss all types of today's functional, less functional, or even dysfunctional families; instead, the goal is to provide some hints for making any family interactions more helpful to the schoolchildren.

Family and work stresses

There are many divergent scenarios with regards to working parents.

For example, often both parents of a student work outside the home. In this case, the working parents may express unease with the time away from home and hence, limited time with their children; they may even blame any difficulties their children are experiencing at school on their absence. Although there may be a correlation between limited parent–child interactions and poor school grades, most of the time children of either dual or single working parents do just as well or even better at school as those families with a parent at home.

In other instances, at least one parent is working at home. Perhaps a parent *must* work at home with a special needs child or may choose to be at home for home schooling. Or perhaps a parent works from a home office so as to have a more flexible arrangement that may benefit the children. In cases such as these, the parent is usually focused, concerned, and aware of the educational curriculum; he or she typically does an excellent job of instructing the child. The parent is "working" from the home.

The point is that whether parents work outside the home or not, or are at home all the time or seldom, children can — and usually do — do well at school.

Parents who work present an entirely different image for their offspring than those who don't work, and that image is positive whether the work is in or out of the home. Teachers should become familiar with the many ways in which working parents present positive role models for their children. If they encounter parents who may feel concerned or worried, they can share the ideas which are outlined in Formula Five: Encouraging Words for Working Parents. Doing so should reduce anxiety and self-reproach.

Insist on quality time.
Share the load.
Be a "happiness" role model.
Network.
Share the budget.

You and Me Date

Here is a variation on Me & You time you might find an opportunity to share.

I once knew a single mom who worked so hard she felt she never had any one-on-one time with her three children. To make up for this, she arranged to take Friday afternoons off. Once a month, she pulled each of her children out of school. Together, they attended a matinee and went for dinner. The fourth Friday, she shared with me, was for her alone. Everyone benefited. The key to making You and Me Date successful is keeping the date at all costs. The child must come first!

Formula Five: Encouraging Words for Working Parents

Insist on quality time. Positive quality time with the child is better than a lot of not-so-positive quantity time. A loving single-parent family is more valuable to a child than a dysfunctional family with two parents. How can parents communicate love in the family? Although we all think we know much about how to do it, sometimes it's difficult to pinpoint specific ways to identify these characteristics. The following list shares ideas for communicating within-family "love."

- Acknowledge the child when he or she enters a room. Look up, make eye contact, smile.
- Use the "shoulder squeeze" for kids who are not at a hugging stage.
- Express pride in and appreciation for little accomplishments, such as learning to recite a short poem. Do so regularly.
- Once in a while, bring home or prepare a little treat, perhaps a new pen or a batch of favorite cookies.
- When the child wants you to listen, be there 100 percent. Stop what you are doing and give uninterrupted one-on-one time for at least five minutes.
- Verbally and regularly express your feelings of affection.

Even a few minutes a day spent together in caring, talking, and sharing can keep children heading in the right direction. A parent might adopt the practice of Me & You time, a 5 to 15 minute time set aside every day, maybe just before bed, during which a child is given all of the parent's attention. Neither parent nor child should "skip" the time.

Share the load. With the children, create plans in which all areas of daily living are outlined and addressed. Give children responsibility for particular tasks, such as doing dishes or vacuuming, as well as for personal grooming. Consistently carry out your responsibilities, as indicated by the chart. Teaching children to find time and take responsibility for aspects of family living is a wonderful gift to give.

Be a "happiness" role model. You are the best role model your child can have. Even though life may be tough, and you may feel burdened and overwhelmed, by consciously looking for the positive and expressing happiness for small things, you will be modeling a "way of existing" immeasurably better than that modeled by parents who are always complaining.

Network. Seek out help and support. Make connections with neighbors, relatives, friends, teachers, coaches, and leaders of children's clubs (e.g., Boy Scouts), groups (reading groups), and teams (after-school soccer). Ask for help with driving kids to and from activities, with shopping, and with childcare. Help others when you can.

Share the budget. Make the family budget a family concern as much as possible given the ages of the offspring. This point is particularly important for families caught up in the anxieties related to these economic times, as described below. Talking honestly with the children about financial matters, while pointing out how and where they can help, will allow a parent, single or otherwise, to relieve any fears. Children sense parents' anxieties, and if these are money based, the youngsters will know, with the usual result being an escalation of worries in their own minds. Better to tell them the situation and invite their help. List the budget limitations (e.g., no new runners until spring or looking for clothes at the local thrift store), together with what they might do as a family. ("Instead of exchanging bought Christmas gifts, let's make personal gifts this year.") Kids respond favorably to this type of approach; they quickly see themselves in responsible roles.

Simple Gifts: A Teacher Initiative

You can help students, especially those living "on a budget," create fantastic gifts for family members. Ever since a seven-year-old approached me with the request, I made the easy making of handmade bookmarks a class staple.

1. Cut a sheet of heavy paper, light cardboard, or sheet of water paint paper, into rectangles about 6 inches by 1.5 inches or the size of a bookmark. One sheet usually makes 10 to 12 bookmarks.
2. Each child decorates one side of the bookmark with crayons, paints, or whatever medium is chosen.
3. On the back is written a short comment to the recipient of the bookmark: "For Mom, because I love you and you like to read," together with date and name of creator: "2010, Love Kelly."
4. Laminate bookmarks; place 10 or 12 side-by-side in the laminator then cut them apart.
5. Punch holes in the tops of the bookmarks, and have students tie ribbon, colored string, embroidery cotton, or such through the hole.

When parents suffer economy-based anxieties

Worried parents tend to lead to worried children.

Today's teachers need to be aware that economic situations may well arise in their classrooms and should be prepared to offer some sort of assistance. Here are a few basic facts to consider.

- First, the responsibilities of child rearing on a single parent can be overwhelming. It has been documented that single parents are more frequently in the lower income bracket and suffer from more health problems. Both of these points can take a toll on offspring.
- Second, with the extensive economic downsizing today, many families are living under extreme tension. Jobs are being lost or shared, mortgages or loans are being refused by financial institutions, savings are being exhausted, and so on. Parents feel overwhelmed. Children feel this anxiety, and parents may be rightfully worried that it is negatively affecting their school performance.
- Third, according to statistics, the gap between the haves and have-nots is widening, creating a problem in many classrooms with greater numbers of children coming to school without necessary supplies, such as pencils. Their parents are struggling to maintain a particular lifestyle in the face of lower incomes that do not keep up with the rate of economic inflation.

Understanding these situations allows the teacher to provide more support for the student(s) from these families, perhaps a bit more individual assistance and reinforcement, and some school-based financial aid if needed (e.g., for field trips and supplies).

In addition, the teacher should be ready to provide words of support which, coming from a concerned teacher, can make all the difference to struggling parents who might be feeling they aren't doing enough for their children. Share with them the points in the previous Formula Five, in particular "Insist on quality time" and "Share the budget." These overtaxed parents may well have heard words of encouragement before, but coming from a teacher, a professional with whom they entrust their children, they can be very comforting.

Dealing with Parents Who Harbor Unreasoning Fears

Parents are perhaps the most affected by threats to peaceful existence. A fear always increases when children are involved, and our current "epidemic of fear" is having negative repercussions on children. The problem all comes down to the idea that in order to become self-sufficient, independent, and productive, one must be allowed to take risks and make mistakes; however, when the risks are magnified by media and pose a threat to personal security, the big picture changes dramatically. Suddenly, teachers find themselves facing many students who are lacking in self-confidence, self-determination, and problem-solving strategies; who, rather than growing in autonomy, are becoming co-dependent with caregivers. This unhealthy development is leaving many educators at a loss as to how to turn it around in their students.

Think back 20 or even 10 years. Although there were, as today, many different sorts of neighborhoods, and many parents escorted their children to and from school like today, there were also many children who walked freely and alone to and from school, from the homes of neighbors and playmates, from games and practices. They rode city transit to the malls or even all the way across cities to visit friends or relatives. They played in parks after school and even, heaven forbid, until after dark.

Enter the era of fear, where danger seems to be lurking everywhere all the time. The word "predator" has taken on a new and eerie definition. Even worse are the feelings that jump to the fore at the word "pervert" and worse yet: "pedophile." No wonder parents are scared — the media have indoctrinated them to believe in a whole new era of rapidly rising risks and fears. No wonder they drive their offspring everywhere, insist on constant and continual contact by cell phone, and prohibit outdoor activities unless they are there as security guards. No wonder kids seem afraid to do, to try, to go anywhere on their own. To be fair, parents who choose to ignore potential threats to their children, as notified by schools or police, would be negligent — here, I am not referring to those conscientious parents, but to the others who have become so frightened they refuse to let children out of their sight — ever.

After talking in depth about this situation with several teachers, I developed the following list of student attributes they felt were the direct results of parent reactions and overreactions. Students in today's troubled times tend to be

- lacking in confidence and decision-making abilities
- unable to solve even minor problems alone
- overly suspicious to the point of paranoia around strangers
- lazy; don't want to walk if they can ride, climb stairs if there's an elevator, or do anything that they might be able to get their parents to do (e.g., canvass neighbors to inform them of an upcoming school event)
- openly and overly afraid of situations over which they have no control, such as world wars, terrorism, disease, poverty, school shootings, and abductions
- more interested in playing (video, computer) games alone than playing with a group; hence, poor socialization skills

Although not all students exhibit these negative traits, enough of them do to make teachers concerned. The fears of today have caused a serious dilemma. On the one hand, they are born from reality and students need to be aware of and prepared for potential threats. On the other hand, their very nature presents a huge roadblock to the natural emergence of self-sufficiency in students, and consequently a massive problem for teachers trying to teach to that very independence.

Parents cannot be faulted; children, who so readily contract their parents' fears, cannot be faulted. The fault, if it must be assigned, lies with a troubled society wherein personal safety has become a valuable commodity and with the media that use fear to make money.

What can teachers do? There is no pat answer, but there are a few ideas that can be employed to help make the entire situation less debilitating to children. These ideas focus on the fearful parents and are for sharing at parent–teacher conferences or meetings, where a parent is open to discussion about personal fears and potential effects on children. I do not advocate that teachers try to force parents to let their anxieties go but rather that teachers offer support and possible guidance for dealing with the fears and the children.

Talking to fearful parents

- Support their beliefs; avoid arguing or trying to point out the "unreasoning" character of their fears.
- Legitimize their fears by talking about the reasons behind them. "I agree there have been many newscasts about the horrible incident at ___school where some children were killed."
- To ensure you understand, address the area of most concern: "I think that what you are most afraid of is the possibility of ___being abducted while she is walking to or from school, and that's why you drive her even when that makes you late for work."
- Have available any data that supports the fact that the chance of such an incident occurring at your school is incredibly small; at the least, encourage parents to think in this vein with a question such as, "What do you think are the chances of something like that ever happening here?" The goal is to promote awareness of the minuscule possibility and thus possibly shift the fear from unreasoning to realistic.
- Suggest the excellent book *Risk*, by Dan Gardner, which deals in detail with these sorts of concerns.
- Be prepared to point out any child weaknesses that may be related to the parent's fear (e.g., fear to go out for recess). "She keeps watching the street and if someone is walking by, she panics." Or, for less obvious behavior, such as lack of independence on the part of the child where she cannot make a decision or solve a minor problem on her own, say something like "I know it's hard to put these two things together, but do you think ___'s dependence on you could be having some effect on her in general? At school she . . ."
- Be prepared with possible alternatives or suggestions. Teachers are viewed as authorities — never leave a parent with a concern that you can't offer some form of hope for remedying. "Maybe you could drop ___ off a couple of blocks from school and let her walk alone while you watch."
- Share with parents all the ways in which your school and, in particular, your class are dealing with personal safety issues (see Putting Safety First, page 85).

As a teacher, be sure to remember that the fears of parents are based on love and concern for their children. Some parents could do more for their children by not doing so much. Of course, the same could be said of some teachers. Children need to experiment, to make mistakes, to fall down repeatedly, yet sometimes it's just so much easier and quicker to "do it for them" than to do damage control

Good Idea

Purchase your own copy of *Risk* and keep it handy for sharing with parents, peers, or anyone who seems to be succumbing to an unreasoning fear.

after the fact. The whole "rescuing" idea is tough for many parents and educators to deal with. We care about the children and want to rescue them from any situation that might prove distressing, yet if we do so, we are suggesting that we don't trust them and that they aren't capable enough, strong enough, or smart enough. Henry Horne says it all: "An infallible way to make your child miserable is to satisfy all his demands."

If you are dealing with a number of fearful parents, you may consider initiating a parent support group whose goal is the sharing of parental concerns with an eye on ways to reduce them. Your role would be that of mediator, and perhaps of organizer as to time and place, at least initially. Keep in mind, however, the tendency of people in groups to support and reinforce previously established beliefs. In other words, when people share a belief and come together to discuss it, the group tends to polarize, to move more to one extreme with the result usually being heightening of the original belief together with the formation of huge biases. It is almost as if the human mind seeks to embrace only information that supports a decision already made and to reject information that counters it. You, the teacher-as-mediator, therefore, must be prepared to offer honest, sincere information and may even need to see about having another professional, perhaps a social psychologist, in attendance. The parent support group is not for the faint of heart and I offer it as a possibility only.

Supporting All Types of Families

Teachers can employ in-class strategies to support all manner of family dynamics and promote egalitarianism among children. Although teachers have always supported family life (it is part of the Social Studies curriculum), given the variety of families and living conditions today, they may have to look outside the curriculum for assistance. The following suggestions may help.

Strategies for supporting parents and family life

- *Literature at Large:* Share children's literature based on a variety of families and divergent lifestyles. A good jumping-off spot is *Clive Eats Alligators* by Alison Lester, a picture book that draws attention to the fact that every child is different in some way. Use the read-aloud or shared reading approach to allow for management of discussion and interjection of questions. (In shared reading, each student can see what the teacher reads aloud whether it be an individual book, photocopied sheets, or visual access to the text via overhead, Power-Point, or flip charts.) There are many great books on family dynamics. If a student asks a question about a sensitive issue, as in "Why does Jenny have two moms?" the teacher must be prepared to respond; otherwise, there would be an implication that something is wrong or unacceptable. Having a ready supply of personal picture books can be a lifesaver at these times. (Books that are sensitive in content are marked with * in the Good Reads following this section.)
- *Parents as Role Models:* Lead class discussions about parents as role models by asking questions such as "What does your mom (or dad) do that you do too?" Encourage students to think of all the ways they "model" their parents. They may well suggest some less-than-positive ways. In this case, try to get the student to come to the realization that maybe in this instance he could find a different approach. For instance, when a boy explained that he swore when he made a mistake because his dad did, he was able to point out that there was a better approach — in this case, he shouted a nonsense word.

"That's Nothing" Motivator

This good activity allows students to poke fun at parts of life that irritate them. It will get them thinking about how everyone has things in life considered "bad."

Break the class into groups of 4 or 5. You may want to establish a theme — in this example, it's "family." Each player takes a turn in sequence trying to offer something that shows how she or he is "worse off" than the previous person.

A: My family is so small that there aren't enough of us to do the work and I get stuck with everything.

B: That's nothing. My family is so big we can't all sit at the table to eat.

C: That's nothing. My family never goes out together because our car is too small.

D: That's nothing. My family yells at the television all the time.

- *Parents as Guests:* Invite parents from all walks of life and family dynamics to visit the class and share stories of how they cope or how their family life may be different from others'. For this "very special guest" day, teacher enthusiasm will set the stage for total acceptance of many family styles.

- *All Families Everywhere:* Bring articles or stories to class that show families from other cultures or countries, perhaps where extended families all live under one roof or where family dynamics are radically different from those of North American families. Present and post pictures or posters illustrating different families from around the world. Many sites online offer posters like this. Or, if you have access to a poster store, check it out for family posters too. I don't suggest spending personal money; if the school budget doesn't allow for this, perhaps you could invite older students or art students to create posters for you.

- *Family Focus Writing:* Provide a writing assignment focused on "how my family is perfect." Try to stay away from "my family troubles" and the like. The goal is to focus on the positive.

- *Play Family Focus:* This discussion game is played in groups of 4 or 5. Each student in turn speaks about his or her family according to the theme provided by the teacher. After each member has shared, the group discusses the similarities and differences between families. Sample theme: One thing your family does together every weekend. Other possible themes include one place visited, one special day, one problem solved, and one room in the house.

- *Family Life Role Play:* Present possible family situations and invite groups to work out brief skits or improvisations depicting them. Examples of possible situations include the family deciding where to go for a vacation, how to spend an unexpected windfall, and what to set as an appropriate penalty for not meeting curfew. The goal is for kids to see that all families approach the same situation in different ways, and all ways are acceptable for the family that uses them. In other words, there is no 100 percent right or perfect way to solve the potential problems.

- *Opposite Options:* Teach and practise Opposite Options, a great activity that many families adopt for at-home use. Opposite Options involves consciously stopping a negative behavior and substituting an opposite behavior; for example, instead of shouting, whisper. Students like this challenge; they call it "op-op," pronounced /aw-p, aw-p/. A Grade 6 class came up with the following list of opposite options.

"Op-op, Op-op"

At a parent–teacher conference, a mother shared that she'd been "in a state" the previous day when she couldn't find her car keys. She had been "ranting and raving" about the stupidity of it when her son calmly said, "Op-op, Mom, op-op." She said she started to laugh and the situation was defused. Unfortunately, she still couldn't find her keys, but at least the negative tension was gone.

Instead of	Try
screaming	whispering
punching	patting
fighting	hugging
crying	singing to self (e.g., "Twinkle, Twinkle")
blaming	repeating a mantra
kicking	dancing
getting angry	sitting down and holding breath

Putting Safety First

All schools have safety programs that teachers will support and reinforce, but individual classrooms can have safety features too. Especially in the earlier grades, Kindergarten to Grade 4, safety-first routines or measures are important and can be shared with parents. Maybe once some of these suggestions are employed, parents can take a small "letting-go" step and allow their children to get to and from school alone. The suggestions, presented in a Formula Five, appear here because their effectiveness is based on parental support and assistance.

Walking "buds."
Transit groupies.
Playground mini-police.
Walking train.
Direct-route map.

Formula Five: Safe Transferring

Walking "buds." Every student is assigned a walking "bud" to walk to and from school with. You as the teacher and instigator of the plan can work this out according to where students live. In some cases, three students might be grouped. If some students are more isolated, obviously other options must be considered. It is the responsibility of the walking "bud" (buddy) to send or receive either a phone call or an e-mail as soon as both buddies are home. This practice serves as a safety precaution in case a child gets accidentally locked out, even though somebody may be at home. A parent or caregiver ensures that the "bud" calls.

Transit groupies. Students who take the same bus are formed into "transit groupies." Like the walking "buds," they need to get in touch with one another by phone or e-mail as soon as they get home. They may wish to take turns serving as a contact person who, for a week, makes the quick home contact. The parent or caregiver of the contact person ensures that the calls are made as soon as the child gets home. Parents can also be put in charge of organizing the transit groupies.

Playground mini-police. These students are assigned by you or other teachers to assist during recess, lunch breaks, and pre- and post-school in the area surrounding the school for a week. Basically, their role is to be alert to suspicious persons or vehicles, and to watch for younger students who may be lingering, then to report to the supervising teacher(s). Teachers always supervise these areas, but having a few more pairs of eyes to help is great; acting as mini-police is a powerful way to promote self-confidence in the involved students. Parents will be notified if their child is going to serve; their responsibility is to discuss this with the child and reinforce the sensible measures taken by the child while "on duty."

Walking train. If a group of young children in Kindergarten to Grade 1 all live in a common area (e.g., same block or court), and have parents or guardians at home after school, they can be grouped for walking. Explain that, like a train, where people get off at different stops, students will get off at their stops only — they will avoid "riding the train" somewhere else. When only two children are left "on the train," they go together to the home of the second-last child, where that parent or caregiver (the "caboose") then walks the final child home. If, at the second-last stop, no parent is yet home, both children wait until a parent arrives to become the caboose. Of course, this practice requires cooperation from the second-last parent, but it is such an excellent and safety-in-numbers approach to transferring that parents readily help out. It may be possible to vary the route so parents take turns as the caboose or arrange for a child to "get off at a different stop" if a parent knows she will not be home. Young children readily adopt the walking train concept and will follow it religiously.

Direct-route map. Children can draw and illustrate the most exact route they can take to and from school. These maps do not have to be to scale. The main thing is to enable students to visualize the best direct routes and follow them. You (or adults aides) may have to help by downloading city maps and sharing hard copies with the students. The final maps should include important places (e.g., post office, corner store) along the way.

Sometimes, just the act of drawing the direct route brings its importance to the fore and encourages its constant use. Parents' responsibility is to check the direct route for accuracy and to reinforce its regular use.

At all times teachers and parents must work together to ensure student safety. Discussions of power walking versus dawdling, for instance, can take place both at school and at home. Open lines of communication will make any safety-first plan work.

Helping Students by Helping Their Parents

Teachers teach towards independence. It's a paradox that they teach their students not to need them, but that's exactly what good teachers do.

Parents also want their children to be independent — someday; unfortunately not all parents see the big picture and inadvertently interfere with children's growth towards independence. Herein lies the teacher–parent conflict.

It's easy to see why some parents are overprotective. Trouble appears to lurk behind every corner. Children can't be allowed out of sight for even a moment for fear of abduction. They can't go swimming in case of drowning. They can't ride a bus in case of poor driving. They can't go on a sleepover in case the other parents are not supervising closely enough. The list goes on. With the media constantly throwing fear in our faces, concerned parents are the norm, and overprotective parents are appearing more frequently.

The result? Less-than-confident kids.

Consider what happens when an adult intervenes and helps a child with something even before it is a problem and certainly before the child experiences any unrest. This well-meaning adult, be it parent, teacher, or someone else, is hurting the child by suggesting, albeit involuntarily, that the child is incapable of handling the situation. The message is clear: "You can't do this without me." In a world where independence and problem-solving abilities are so important for ultimate happiness and success, the child is being robbed of a valuable opportunity for personal growth in that direction. If this happens repeatedly, well, you can see the picture.

Finding the Best Route

Once I witnessed a child creating a direct-route map based on the way he had been traveling home: it was the most circuitous route possible. After discussing the matter with him, I realized he didn't know any other route and was following the roads his mom took in the car. His mom, however, always stopped at various grocery stores, mailboxes, and so forth on the way home. Together, we found a better direct route and walked it together the first time.

The adults are rescuing; they are jumping in to "save" when what they really need to do is provide support. Teachers can see their actions more objectively. They are usually aware that they are "rescuing" and hence can control this behavior. Not so with parents. Too often today, teachers are faced with students who have been so overprotected that they are virtually unable to take even little steps on their own; who are fearful, mistrusting, suspicious of others, and maybe even a bit paranoid. To help these students, teachers must help their parents.

The following suggestions are offered for teachers who want to help their students by first helping their parents. Not all suggestions need be used with all parents. It's up to the discerning teacher to choose the ones appropriate for specific situations.

Suggestions for teachers helping parents

In a private discussion you might share these ideas with parents. Be discreet and accept their stances without judging or arguing. Rather, make a few suggestions, give support, and try to focus on the welfare and future of the child. The following are strategies the parents can implement. Your part is to sustain them in their attempts and report any visible, positive changes you see in their children. You, too, should employ these strategies at school.

- **Allow mistakes.** Sometimes parents need reminding that it's okay, good even, to allow their children to make mistakes, to fail. For parents well grounded in the "rescuing" mode, this lesson is tough. This problem can be huge and if the parent(s) cannot see it in its entirety, it may even require intervention from a psychologist or school counselor.
- **Avoid perpetual giving.** No one ever gets everything they want in life, so it's erroneous for parents to think that by giving their children everything they ask for, the children will be happy. Remind the parents that having to wait or work for desired items, not getting them at all, or receiving substituted items of more budget-friendly value are realistic and appropriate outcomes. There is a statement by an unknown author that I love: "Parents who are always giving their children nothing but the best usually wind up with nothing but the worst." This proverb is worth sharing with too generous parents during, for example, parent–teacher conferences, or perhaps during the routine phone call that many teachers make monthly.
- **Be aware that children adopt, exaggerate, and internalize adult worries.** If parents are constantly expressing worries about money, war, terrorism, disease, and so on, their children will also worry and to an even greater degree. Because they don't really understand the situations, children embellish the concerns, fantasize them into even more terrifying problems than they already are, and agonize, often in silence so as not to cause further anxiety to parents. The key is to either share the concerns with children, using terms they understand and suggesting positive outcomes, or avoid talking about them when children are within earshot.
- **Don't just trust — give implicit trust.** Parents want to trust their children, but the world with all its dangers is intimidating, frightening, and always ready to take a bite of innocent children. Or so it seems. The teacher can talk to parents about trust, especially implicit trust. Basically, she can say, "Implicit trust for your children means that you trust them to grow up and not need you any more." Few parents would disagree with this statement.

The next comment takes it further: "Implicit trust to become independent has to start now, with the little things, like being allowed to sleep over, to walk two blocks to school, or to be home alone for two hours." This comment can open a discussion about how and when parents trust, and ways in which trust might be expanded. Many parents are not aware that their refusal to allow certain activities demonstrates a lack of trust. Of course, there is always a concern about whether something is a trust or a safety issue. If an unsavory character lives along the route and is usually hanging around outside — a real danger in allowing the child to walk the two blocks — then it is an entirely different situation. In a case like this, the trust can be given elsewhere.

- **Take baby steps.** Once an area of difficulty has been established with parents, such as giving too much, rescuing too often, or not trusting enough, a plan of action involving the taking of baby steps can be initiated. Here, the parents and the teacher can work as partners. Whatever the parent starts at home — for example, permitting the child to walk a short distance alone — the teacher can reinforce at school. In the case of walking alone, the teacher could have the student journal her feelings about this new step in her development towards independence. Parents taking baby steps can be reminded to

> differentiate between trust and safety issues and explain these to the child
> establish boundaries and rules regarding the new level of trust (e.g., no playing with friends on the way home)
> talk about "what if's" (e.g., what if on the way home you realize you forgot something at school and have to go back, and by doing so, you will exceed the time boundaries? What can you do?)
> discuss how this independence can gradually move towards greater independence, such as being able to play in the schoolyard for 15 minutes before starting home

Setting Boundaries

A good boundary would be the time required for the activity (e.g., 10 minutes), coupled with the understanding that if more time is involved, the parent will take some sort of action, such as going to look for the child.

- **Have faith and express confidence.** You will want to remind parents that they can help their children develop self-confidence. They can achieve this by talking to the children and raising them to believe they can be successful, and, of course, by loving them. By listening to, accepting, congratulating and, when necessary, crying with their children, they will succeed at parenting.

As the involved teacher, remember that taking these measures is as much a step towards independence for the parents as for the child. Help ease the family's transition from the child's dependency to a degree of independence. For example, call home when you know the child has arrived the first time and congratulate the parent on letting the child walk alone, or with a friend.

Finally, you might want to share this quotation by Hodding Carter Jr. with parents: "There are two lasting bequests we can give our children. One is roots. The other is wings." A parent smiled when I shared this insight with him and said that he gave his son the roots, but that I had to give his child the wings. I happily assured him that we were partners in the "wing division," and we shared a smile and a handshake.

Discovering Parents as Experts

Although suggestions have been made for helping parents to help their children, teachers need to remember that parents themselves are a valuable resource. They are the experts when it comes to their children, even though many of them put the expert-status on the teacher(s). Teachers can gently remind parents of their innate skills in regard to the students and ask for guidance, if necessary.

A good place to give this reminder is at a parent–teacher interview where the teacher asks for help in dealing with a specific concern, such as in-class distractibility. No doubt the parents see distractibility in the child too, and have suggestions about it. Or, perhaps the distractibility is only at school; in this case, more evidence needs to be gathered by parents and teachers together.

In an actual example, a teacher was having trouble getting a Grade 1 student to sit properly at his desk. He wiggled a lot and always wanted his feet tucked under him. His restlessness caused a lack of focus not only with him, but with nearby students. When the teacher mentioned this to the child's parents, the dad explained that the boy was used to sitting on a small pillow at home (to add height) and that maybe that would work at school too. It did. Problem solved.

Experts in children's eyes

Teachers need to remember to invite ideas from parents. A good way to do this, and make the most of skills parents have, is to create a "Parent-Experts" list with students. This list identifies all areas where parents can be considered the experts — through the eyes of their children anyway. The list could include such things as huggers, drivers, homework helpers, and readers.

Collating a group list gives the teacher an idea not only of how children see their respective parents, but also of which parents might be possible helpers for specific in-class projects. For instance, when a child said his mother was an expert card maker, the teacher invited the mother to class to help the students make Christmas cards and it was a huge success.

Sharing the finished "Parent-Experts" list with parents is useful too, as it reminds parents just how valued they are.

Surveys and invitations

Other ways for teachers to find out about the skills and talents of their students' parents is to send home a simple survey asking them how they might want to contribute to the class. Part of a survey might look like this:

We love to have parents visit our class and share with us exciting, new skills, talents, and ideas. Please check any of the following that you might be able to share with us, and indicate dates and times when you are available.

___ cooking   ___ flower drying   ___ painting (e.g., oil, watercolor)

___ rock collecting ___ dog grooming ___ exercise routine

Teachers can list any topic that interests their students, as well as an "other" point. The example list above is just short, but by offering a comprehensive list, teachers can give parents a better idea of the many areas in which they can assist the class.

There are still other ways teachers can find out about parents as experts. They can include a brief explanation and invitation with the school or class newsletter, display "Expert-Parent" posters at Open House or parent–teacher interviews, send e-mail messages or even make phone calls through a volunteer or an aide.

Parents may often seem beleaguered and stressed, but no one should underestimate how much they can teach and help their children.

Teachers may wish to include the following quotation by Charles R. Swindoll, author of *The Strong Family*, in their communication with parents as experts, as it reminds parents — and themselves — how important parents' influence is, even in the classroom:

"Each day of our lives we make deposits in the memory banks of our children."

CHAPTER 5

Concerning New-Age Teachers

"When you become a teacher, you turn into a manager of this whole system. You become the person controlling the bubble of innocence around a child, regulating it."
— Kazuo Ishiguro

There is nothing I can say about teachers or teaching that hasn't been said many times before. The best I can hope to do is reawaken resourcefulness, stimulate creativity, and reopen doors to a little magic.

Teachers are not immune to today's troubled times. In fact, more than any other professionals, they may struggle and bend under the weight of our chaotic world, for they not only deal with their own anxieties, but those of their students and their students' parents as well. Teachers, like everyone else, worry about job security, personal safety, economic recession, world poverty, famine, natural disasters, and all manner of crises. And because teachers are compassionate and caring by nature, they bear the burdens with heavy hearts. Yet, every day they must walk into their classrooms and face captive audiences with smiles and good will. They must put on their "teacher faces," no matter how they are feeling or what thoughts, worries, or fears lie heavy in their heads and hearts. Not an easy task. Not a task for the faint of heart. Not a task to take lightly.

Often, students and even some parents don't think of teachers as being like everybody else. Teachers are seen as paragons of virtue, of knowledge, of wisdom, of endless ideas, and of unconditional support. Since they *teach* all the other professions, they are surely members of the first and most important profession. Teachers, students believe, are not quite human. Amusing as this perception seems, there may be some truth to it. For 6 to 10 hours a day, teachers maintain a facade that is unbiased, unburdened with personal trepidation or concerns, and yet completely open and receptive to the pains, worries, fears, and upsets of their students. These are *über*-humans. A seven-year-old once told me that all teachers were "aliens" — I hope he meant it in a positive way. In retrospect, I have to agree with him; teachers face such daunting challenges with doubtless smiles that they may very well be aliens.

Yet these *super* humans have as many personal fears, dilemmas, and anxieties as the rest of the population. They must deal with them differently, though. They have to handle their personal issues in such a way as to not upset their students or their students' parents, while dealing with the fears, dilemmas, and anxieties of everyone in their charge. How do they do this? Obviously, they have to skillfully compartmentalize their heads and hearts so as to remain predictably calm in the classroom. Of course, I do not suggest that teachers be emotionless robots — quite the opposite. But their private worries and apprehensions, quite probably escalated in today's troubled times, must be locked away each morning when they open the classroom doors. Sometimes doing this is a Herculean task, compounded by the equally difficult task of teaching in 2010 and beyond. Much research has gone into helping teachers help students; not so much has focused on helping teachers help themselves. My intent is that some of the ideas in this chapter will speak to that area.

With that in mind, how do teachers, already burdened with anxiety springing naturally from today's troubles, find the energy and spark to assuage students' fears while prompting them to pay attention to seemingly mundane information and to learn? What magic can teachers employ to free anxious little minds from troubling world issues that are really too big, too nasty, and too overwhelming for them? How can these concerned educators motivate their students to pay attention in the face of adversity?

Similarly, how do teachers find the time and energy to deal with their own troubles when their days are already over full? Where do the fresh teaching strategies or motivators come from when there isn't time to ruminate, think imaginatively, or explore the incalculable information on the Internet? What happens when a teacher finds herself questioning her position, her profession, her philosophy? And what about "teacher burnout"? I hate to use those words; they imply some sort of evil end. I would rather talk about teachers' need for battery boosts — every single teacher has had, or will have, this all-prevailing need. There have been myriad books, articles, Internet sites, television broadcasts, and so on about this timely topic. Why, then, am I mentioning it here? Because it is such a real and current issue, and this book provides at least some of that help, by considering motivational strategies, teaching philosophies, ways to "distance" self from students, suggestions for dealing with personal tragedies and grief, ideas to help prevent teacher-battery-drain, hints for reducing curriculum overload, and possible teacher responses to today's tough, anxiety-laden questions.

Getting Grounded in a Teaching Philosophy

Do all teachers question their professional choice? I believe they do, at times. And I believe they need to revisit and rewrite their professional goals and objectives periodically. Given the turmoil in teaching today, this revisiting and rewriting may need to be carried out more often so that teachers' philosophies of education are in accordance with life in our modern world.

In my first year of teaching when I was asked to write my personal philosophy of teaching, I was lost. The manuscript ended up being a rather ridiculous tribute to every professor I had at university. It was verbose, ambiguous, and rambling. It said nothing of the way I feel about the profession today. It made me *think*, however — and that's the real purpose of expressing your teaching philosophy. A philosophy has other values as well. In today's world of upheaval, of chaos, of failing economies, of fear, hate, and sorrow, of too few supplies and too many students per class, it is important to figure out why you are a teacher and what you hope to accomplish. I am suggesting that, if you haven't already done so, you make the time to write a teaching philosophy that truly reflects you: a teacher in today's world. If you wrote a philosophy several years ago, upon reassessment you may well find that your philosophy is different today. That's perfectly okay; in fact, it *should* be different today because teaching is different today.

Here is an example. A new teacher's philosophy contained the belief that she would "treat every student the same way all the time." After 10 years of teaching, several of them in a special needs classroom, the teacher confided to me that her philosophy had changed drastically. She now believes firmly that children should be treated differently; they need to be treated individually according to their specific strengths and weaknesses. When I questioned this by pointing out that she still seemed to treat all her students with equal compassion and respect, she agreed, but explained that in her original philosophy she had been referring to so much more, such as time spent with each, amount of assistance given each, challenges provided each, and so on. Her teaching philosopy had altered with experience.

I appreciate that time is valuable. Teachers don't have an extra hour — *ever* — to sit and do something as seemingly frivolous as write a personal teaching philosophy that is relevant to and dependent upon a world that seems bent on self-destruction and inhospitable to easy instruction of the young. However, I am suggesting you do that anyway, for a number of reasons.

Reasons for writing a "current" teaching philosophy

- Writing this will clarify your goals as a teacher. These goals are variable. They should change regularly to adapt to a rapidly changing world and changing curriculum; if you established your goals some time ago, they may well be inappropriate for this new decade.
- It will revisit and reinforce your personal reasons for being a teacher.
- It may very well kindle a dying spark for the profession, especially if you simplify the goals into reachable targets.
- It helps you to see what you expect from your students, what changes you hope they will exhibit.
- It reminds you of, or makes changes to, personal traits you want to demonstrate in the classroom.

A philosophy does not have to be long, detailed, or even professionally written. It is a letter of intent to you, from you. It is a worthwhile endeavor, especially today when, I believe, the profession of teaching is difficult and fraught with problems.

Guidelines for writing a "today" philosophy of teaching

My current philosophy consists of three sentences only:

> Learning should be fun. The key to *fun* learning, the stance I must take is to provide effective communication, a socially constructive environment, a passionate and exciting outlook, and a caring, supportive, accepting attitude. My students will be encouraged to be independent learners who are curious, motivated, and self-confident.

My original philosophy was much longer and contained many rather puffed-up ideals, such as being a good role model, keeping current by being involved in ongoing self-education, maintaining an educational network, and so on. The way my philosophy is written now allows me to access and re-access it quickly. I can write a checklist of traits and scrutinize them easily.

While short, my current philosophy encompasses my firm beliefs about teaching. It works better for me than a two- or three-page document filled with jargon and impossible goals. When I feel frustrated and discouraged, I return to my philosophy and remind myself that nowhere does it say I must save every child or even "make" every child learn. It reminds me that, above all, learning should be fun. So, I suggest keeping your teaching philosophy handy for quick reference when the troubles of today make you wonder why you ever chose this profession.

Assuming that you do decide to write — or rewrite — your teaching philosophy, here are a few guidelines.

It's a good idea to determine just what sort of a teacher you are. Robert Frost wrote, "There are two kinds of teachers: the kind that fill you with so much quail shot that you can't move, and the kind that just gives you a little prod behind and you jump to the skies." The following list of teacher types has been compiled from various sources, including students. Which teacher type are you? Answer honestly by checking the attributes that apply.

☐ Happy ☐ Funny ☐ Fun ☐ Friendly ☐ Serious ☐ Supportive ☐ Caring
☐ Honest ☐ Intelligent ☐ Helpful ☐ Dramatic ☐ Lenient ☐ Fair
☐ Hardworking ☐ Strict ☐ Dedicated ☐ Calm ☐ Excited

How many did you check? Every one of these traits can be found in the best teachers; however, we all have personal styles, characteristics that are more prevalent than others when we teach. With the teacher-types list, my best suggestion is that if there were traits you didn't view as part of your teaching style, these might be areas on which to work to improve your teaching effectiveness. The attributes that most suit you — that are most *like* you — should guide the writing of your teaching philosophy.

Too often, the general public fails to value the work of teachers, but this quotation from Dan Rather speaks for those who do: "The dream begins with a teacher who believes in you, who tugs and pushes and leads you to the next plateau, sometimes poking you with a sharp stick called 'truth.'" Value your profession; value your contribution and the way you choose to tug and pull students to the next level, and write that into your personal philosophy.

The following Formula Five provides a few suggestions to help you create a meaningful philosophy.

Define learning.
Determine your approach.
Assess personal traits.
Project student outcome(s).
Determine desired student traits.

Formula Five: Writing a Personal Philosophy of Teaching

Define learning. Think of one or two words that explain what learning means to you or what you want it to mean to the students you meet. What should learning be? For me, the single word "fun" captured it all.

Determine your approach. What will you do, and do to the best of your ability, to help this goal become as much a reality as possible? Try to be specific. For me, the best strategy was good communication skills.

Assess personal traits. You know yourself. And you know that *what* you are — perhaps a person of sincere warmth with a love of kids — is more important than what you *teach*. What positive traits do you bring to the job or would you like to bring if you do not already? These may be traits you need to work on or traits you already have. For me, the important traits were being passionate, caring, supportive, and accepting. As a novice teacher, I didn't have these traits, but I knew I needed them if I was to reach my goal of finding that "education is fun." I love this wonderful quotation by Carl Jung: "One looks back with appreciation to the brilliant teachers, but with gratitude to those who touched our human feelings. The curriculum is so much necessary raw material, but warmth is the vital element for the growing plant and for the soul of the child."

Project student outcome(s). What single goal would you wish for your general student body? For some teachers, that is to "learn and pass the grade." For some it is to "like school." It doesn't matter what your philosophy is; what matters is that you have a goal and are aware of what you want your students to do, know, or be. My goal has always been for students to learn without me, to learn independently.

Determine desired student traits. What traits do you want students to cultivate? Some teachers want students to be quiet, dedicated, and respectful. Some want them to be outgoing, assertive, and playful. Again, there are not right or wrong choices; every teacher takes a personal position. In my case, I wanted to nurture curiosity and confidence.

Motivating New-Age Students

As previously mentioned, an area of concern for teachers today is that of student motivation. Of course, this has always been an education issue; students don't learn unless they want to learn. It's up to teachers to make them want to learn. Surely, to paraphrase Horace Mann, a teacher who is attempting to teach without inspiring the student with a desire to learn is hammering on cold iron. However, too often teachers find themselves "hammering on cold irons." One cause is that they have to compete with the latest "techie toys" — often a losing battle. This is especially true when it comes to struggling students who may be turned off from education by the time they reach a classroom.

One frustrated teacher confided, "There is nothing I can do to motivate them any more. Tricks that used to work don't work. All they are interested in is the high-tech stuff. How do I compete with that? How do I make spelling interesting when they all text in phonics?"

How indeed? The best response I have is to include brief motivating activities into daily routines. These activities should stop inappropriate behaviors, refocus attention, and allow the teacher to maintain control over the classroom. I have written a book, *Three Minute Motivators*, filled with such ideas, but because I believe so firmly in their worth, I will include several of them here.

Any of the following motivators can be used at any time during a day or a class to recapture attention, help reduce excess energy, or provide a positive time-out for students and teachers. These little breaks serve as mini-rest periods or emotional breathers; for some students they even relieve stress. The key is to make them games, fun activities without pressures to perform or fears of losing. Your attitude will convey this to the students. Smile and enjoy! That's all you require to make anytime motivators successful. Leo F. Buscaglia wrote, "It is paradoxical that many educators and parents still differentiate between a time for learning and a time for play without seeing the vital connection between them." Let's use games, motivators, surprises, and "fun stuff" to reinforce that integral connection between learning and play.

At-seat motivators involving pencil and paper

- *Dotty Designs:* Partners (*A* and *B*) fold a single sheet of blank paper in quarters. *A* draws about 10 dots randomly in one quarter while *B* keeps eyes closed. *A* closes eyes and *B* draws dots on a different quadrant. They do the same thing once more so that there are random dots in each quadrant. They open the page and then work together to join the dots to make some sort of visual image. All dots must be used and more than one image can be drawn as long as the images "fit" together (e.g., a sun and a house).

   Follow-up: Name the finished art and share it with peers, explaining the title.

After each anytime motivator is a follow-up suggestion. Follow-ups do not have to be used — the activities are reinforcing on their own — but they are provided in case the teacher wants to take them further.

- *Free-Flow Tales:* Provide partners or small groups with a time-relevant theme, such as sports, winter, or a holiday. *A* begins writing on theme, using proper grammar, sentence construction, spelling, and so on. On your cue, *A* hands the pencil to *B*, who picks up from where *A* left off and writes. No talking is allowed. The idea is to make a coherent story by using what has already been written.

    Follow-up: Share the stories orally. Use them as bases for additional writing.
- *Alphabet Scrabble:* Partners *A* and *B* each randomly choose 10 letters of the alphabet. They jot them down on paper, but keep them hidden from each other. They flip a coin to see who will start, and (in this example) *B* writes one of his 10 letters on a separate page — "k." If she can, *A* then writes down either or both letters adjacent to *B*'s letter, earning one point for one letter and two points for two letters. If *A* doesn't have an adjacent letter on her list, she will have to forfeit, give a point to *B*, and put down any letter. *B* then tries to put down at least one adjacent letter. Plays are alternated until one partner has no letters left. The partner with the most points wins. To review, points are earned when the other partner cannot provide an adjacent letter or when a partner can add one adjacent letter (1 point) or two adjacent letters (2 points; 1 for each letter).

    Follow-up: Any sequencing task, such as using dictionary skills, is a good follow-up.
- *Scribble-Sense:* On your cue, each partner "scribbles" for 15 seconds, trying to use the entire side of separate blank pages. Caution students not to fill in every space but to scribble "gently" (curving and straight lines intersecting). After 15 seconds, partners exchange pages and attempt to make sense of or create a visual image out of the other's scribbles.

    Follow-up: Study art, especially the work of impressionistic or abstract artists, or journal about the results — the "picture" found in the scribbles.
- *Down-to-Earth Definitions:* Small groups (3–5) work together to create amusing, real-life definitions of words (e.g., "pencil" — a thin, wooden instrument, about 4 inches (10 cm) in length, used for scratching the back while seated at your desk). Allow about five words for definition and encourage dictionary-like wording.

    Follow-up: This activity is an excellent prelude to a creative writing assignment. Groups can share their definitions and then individuals can write paragraphs using as many of the unusual definitions as possible in some logical manner. Or, individuals can create posters or illustrations showing many of the unusual definitions in collage form.
- *Twinkle-Twinkle:* Working in pairs or small groups, students change the words of four lines of the popular rhyme "Twinkle, twinkle, little star, How I wonder what you are, Up above the world so high, Like a diamond in the sky." This same activity can be done many times, and students will continue to come up with amusing little rhymes. It usually helps to share one or two to give students the idea. The following are examples from a Grade 5 class:

Twinkle twinkle little pot,	*Purring purring little cat*
I hear you bubbling quite a lot,	*You're all curled up and kind of fat,*
What good stuff do you gently simmer?	*Sitting on that chair you own*
I just can't wait until it's dinner.	*Like a queen upon her throne.*

    Follow-up: Share the poems or save them for later writing assignments.

At-seat motivators involving oral responses

- *Finger Talk:* This is rather like finger puppets without the puppets; somehow by letting fingers do the talking, children are better able to let their inhibitions go and carry on amusing conversations. Partners face each other and make hands into fists with pointer fingers out. The fingers will do the talking by bending, bobbing, and so on as the student speaks. There is no physical interaction between the fingers. You can suggest a theme to talk about (e.g., pet peeves). Usually some sort of grievance, especially if it is a hot topic, such as why homework is assigned on weekends, works well.

  Follow-up: Partners can create a script and skit for peers or share any positive suggestions or results that came from their talk.

- *Buy a Clue:* Within the class and using natural divisions, such as rows and tables, make 3 to 5 groups. Each group gets three tokens with which to buy clues. Tokens can be anything handy, including pencils, erasers, and pennies. You secretly think of a place, perhaps in the room (e.g., the back cupboard) or some place from class studies (e.g., a city mentioned in Social Studies or the home of a narrative protagonist). Randomly select the order in which groups participate through numbers on paper scraps chosen by groups. Group 1 "buys a clue" by exchanging a token for it, and the teacher then provides a clue ("Not in our classroom, but in our city"). Groups are allowed 30 seconds to think together following each clue, then to make a guess if they want to. Each group can make 3 to 5 guesses, depending on your estimate of how difficult it is to find the place. Continue buying and telling clues. Gradually make the clues more specific. The team that guesses the place wins. This game can be played with the whole class against the teacher (or other leader) if desired.

  Follow-up: Discuss how we use clues in everyday life, such as to learn about others. Have students think of clues leading to a "treasure." This type of question-and-answer formation promotes inductive thinking.

- *Cry Me a River:* In small groups (3–5), students take turns "whining." Tell them that a good whiner is not necessarily the loudest but the one that wins the most sympathy votes. It's not all about noise; it's about a whiny voice and string of complaints. After everyone in each group has had a chance to whine, the group selects the "best whiner" to share with the rest of the class. Keep reminding students this is for fun only.

  Follow-up: Students can journal how they feel when others whine. Ask them to recall a time they were whining and write about it, mentioning how others around them might have felt.

- *I Assume:* Students work as partners or in small groups (3–5). In response to a given situation, students discuss what assumptions they come up with based on the information given. After about five minutes, groups share their assumptions and you share the truth of the situation, which should be quite different from most assumptions. Possible situations include these:

  A woman was running as fast as she could to get to a stopped bus.
  	Truth: The woman was the bus driver and was late for work.
  A little boy was sitting on the pavement hugging a tiny dog and crying.
  	Truth: The little boy used to have a stuffed toy that looked like the dog he found on the street. It was his favorite toy and it got lost.
  A very old man was shuffling painfully across the street holding the arm of a young girl.

Truth: The girl was blind and her grandfather was helping her across the street.

Follow-up: Have students discuss with partners any times when they made incorrect assumptions. Together, each pair can write a script about a single incident they can make one up if they don't want to use a personal one. They can then act out or read the script to the class.

- *A Whole for 2 Halves:* Partners brainstorm for compound words (e.g., lifestyle, sandcastle). The teacher gives a start cue and allows brainstorming for 2 or 3 minutes. The pair with the most words wins. A more difficult version is to create compound words that are self-explanatory (e.g., toewalker, snowstars).

  Follow-up: Discuss briefly how new words are coined when there becomes a need for them. For example, in technology, the words "blog," "Facebook," and "Twitter" have quite recently emerged. Alternatively, students can write a story using some of the compound words they listed.

- *Mystery Word:* In this simple cognitive game, the teacher thinks of a word and writes it down secretly. Students randomly ask yes/no questions to try to identify the word. They cannot ask two questions or suggest two answers in a row. Encourage turn-taking. If desired, use a more formal system of turn-taking or hand-raising. The goal is to find the mystery word. Keep track of how long it takes students as a group and challenge them at future times to beat their records. You may wish to provide hints or clues if the students are stuck.

  Follow-up: Have students write questions relevant to a topic of study, a valuable activity for helping kids become independent learners.

- *Tell-a-Tale:* There is nothing quite like storytelling to dispel worry and anxiety, and Tell-a-Tale is storytelling at its best. It begins with a story bag, a small bag in which you have put a collection of interesting items — small plastic doll, little farm animals, broken watch, compass, magnifying glass, toy comb, and so on. Take a quick stroll through a dollar store for infinite ideas. Begin Tell-a-Tale by enthusiastically displaying the Tell-a-Tale bag and using a pat opening phrase such as "Once upon a time, far away and long ago . . ." Always use the same opening when beginning Tell-a-Tale as this sets the stage for what is to come. Say the phrase passionately, then invite a student to reach into the bag and pull out an item. This item then becomes the central figure of the Tell-a-Tale. For instance, a toy horse is pulled. You say, "Once upon a time, far away and long ago, a pretty little horse was running through the fields when all of a sudden . . ." Stop and invite students to raise their hands to continue the story. Once they get going, children are eager to add to the tale. If they get stuck, either allow another item to be pulled from the bag and consequently added to the story, or add an idea yourself.

  Follow-up: Have students use cartoon strips to illustrate the key points in the created story, or have them list on paper 5 to 7 unrelated items and then exchange papers with others and write stories incorporating all the items.

- *The Probability Factor:* This motivator is often used in conjunction with a math lesson, but it stands alone well too. Present a coin and start flipping it to get attention. Then tell students you have flipped it 10 times and that "heads" have shown up every time. You can do this, but don't let them see which side was up. Invite them to guess what will show on the next flip. Most will say "tails" in the incorrect belief that since heads have shown so many times in a row, then surely tails will be next. In fact, there is still a 50/50 chance of it being heads again. Flip and discuss. It doesn't matter whether it shows heads or tails; if you want to, you can use this to lead a discussion about probability and the idea that we have about "shoulds." "Why did we think it would be tails?" "What evidence is there that it would be tails?" On its own, The Probability Factor serves to capture kids' attention and make them think.

Follow-up: Challenge students to find short stories, poems, or even illustrations from magazines or the Internet that might suggest the probability of something happening—perhaps a cartoon of a bike rider headed towards an unseen hole. Almost any situation can be used; the idea is to encourage divergent thinking and imagination.

Motivators involving silent movement

- *Stuck on You:* Groups of 2 or 3 students stand in a safe area, that is, not adjacent to desks or sharp objects. Call out body parts randomly along with random numbers from 1 to 4, and the groups (partners) must stick these parts together. For instance, if you call, "Hands 3," then three hands must be touching. If the next call is "Heads 2," then two heads must also be touching. Be resourceful, but watch students carefully to see that there is some way for them to stick together as suggested. This game is reminiscent of Twister from the 1960s, and the students love it.

  Follow-up: Have students stretch before sitting down again. They can also journal feelings during the game.

- *Air Writing:* Stand with your back to the class and write something in the air, such as "I like you." The students guess what is written. The first to guess correctly becomes the air writer. An alternative is to write directions in the air — for example, "turn around three times" — and have students follow them.

  Follow-up: Instead of making big curvy lines in the air, have students create visualizations with charcoal or paint on large papers.

- *Team Snowflake:* Students work in groups of six; if a group has fewer than six members, it will have to compensate creatively. Remind students that snowflakes have six "arms" and that every snowflake is unique. Allow 2 or 3 minutes for each group to form its snowflake, take a mental picture of it (remember their positions), and then "melt." In turn, each group presents their snowflake. No matter how many times students do this, it remains energizing.

  Follow-up: Create a connection between the individuality of snowflakes and the individuality of the students. Have students write about their own uniqueness.

- *Bubble Brigade:* The goal of this motivator is to blow the maximum number of bubbles in one breath. Students count for each other, and everyone who wants a turn should get a turn. Half the fun is in watching the beautiful bubbles, and often the kids are happy not to blow. Bubble Brigade is one of only two motivators that require a previously obtained product: bubble mixture. Bubble liquid is inexpensive and although it can be homemade, the ready-made product seems to work better and is easy to store. (If, however, you want to make your own bubble mixture, the recipe appears at left.)

  Follow-up: Invite students to find out why bubbles take on rainbow colors, to illustrate bubbles, and to create collages of bubble images. Making a collage involves producing spheres of varying and overlapping sizes by use of water paints or lightly used pencil crayons. Encourage students to cover the entire page, with bubbles disappearing off the pages (that is, with only parts of them

Recipe for Bubble Mixture
½ cup dish soap
(Some work better than others. Experiment. I like "Joy.")
1½ cups warm water
2 tsp sugar
Gently stir (do not shake); keep sealed.

showing). When bubbles overlap, students can experiment with overlapping colors.

- *Silent Commands:* The class forms two teams. (For expediency, draw an imaginary line between halves of the room.) Within each team students pair off into sender and receiver. Each "task" is performed by four people: a pair from each team. Using an overhead or board or large piece of paper, write simple commands that each Team A sender sends to his or her receiver by mouthing the words silently. The Team A receiver and both sender and receiver from Team B cover their eyes or turn their backs so that they do not see the written command. Time how long it takes Team A to complete the task correctly. Then the same task is given to Team B, with only the receiver of B now shielded from seeing the written words. A time is recorded. This constitutes "Round 1."

  Play as many rounds as desired; the team with the fastest record wins. I usually put a limit of 60 seconds to each trial. Some task ideas include standing and turning around or moving to the door on tiptoes.

  Follow-up: Discuss the challenges faced by the hearing impaired, as well as the importance of proper enunciation (with "big mouth" movements).

- *Tai Chi Two:* Students stand beside desks and copy any two large movements demonstrated by you, once you have explained that Tai Chi is a slow-moving form of Eastern exercise. The moves do not have to replicate Tai Chi moves; however, if you are a Tai Chi advocate, by all means make them realistic. Otherwise, use two very different, very big upper body movements (e.g., complete arm circle moving in front of the body and back to hanging loosely at the side, followed by both hands pressed together as if in prayer and moving straight up, then separating at the top and forming two circles). The goal is to get students copying the movements in sequence (you can have more than two if you want), then repeating them over and over *very slowly*. Most students go too quickly. Suggest that they think of "slow motion movies" or "moving through water." The slow, concentrated movements create the sense of well-being.

  Follow-up: Discuss how the movements made the students feel and ask them to journal their feelings.

- *Air Balloons:* This motivator requires balloons. Most of you probably already have these on hand in your desks, but if not, buy them at dollar stores. Divide the class into groups of five. Each group is given a balloon, blows it up as big as possible without breaking it, and knots it. On cue from you, the groups pat the balloons into the air and keep them there by patting them up. No student is allowed to pat two times in a row, so some strategy is involved. Air Balloons can be a who-can-keep-them-up-the-longest? game or simply a game of enjoyment.

  The game can be made more difficult by changing the rules as follows: tap with elbows only, tap twice in a row, tap with left hand only, tap with closed fist, and call the name of the person you are tapping the balloon to.

  Follow-up: Discuss in small groups where, in real life, objects are kept in the air (e.g., planes, air balloons, birds, clouds), and if there is any comparison between them and their balloons. Or, students can journal feelings experienced during the activity.

- *Photocopy Me:* Each group of 4 or 5 gets a turn being the "original" while all others are the "copies." The "original" group works together to form a complicated freeze, or tableau, while members of the other groups have heads on desks, not peeking. (Explain that this is a trust issue.) On cue, the copies are allowed to look carefully at the original for 30 seconds while the tableau is held; then, the original "melts" (comes apart), and the copies have 60 seconds to re-create the original. This activity is not a competition; it is an engaging activity of cooperation and memory.

Follow-up: In the same groups, students can discuss what was easy or difficult about the task, and why this might have been the case (memory, cooperation, observation).

- *Common Calmers:* When students need to calm down, Common Calmers is great. Sitting silently at desks, they simply mime whatever the teacher tells them to, doing the actions slowly, carefully, and paying attention to details as well as to thoughts that may come to them. Common actions that work well are brushing teeth; wiggling toes, then fingers, then noses; clenching and opening hands to fists; opening and squeezing eyes shut; hugging self (wrapping both arms around body) while turning from side to side; gently drawing circles on the forehead using fingers of both hands; massaging the back of the neck with both hands; and stretching the mouth wide open, then shutting. Any action chosen must be repeated over and over again for up to two minutes. Since doing this is quite difficult, shorter periods may need to be used — the calming results are amazing.

Follow-up: Discuss the positive effects of the task and why they seemed positive (or negative if some children saw them thus; obviously, there is no right or wrong). Suggest that students try this technique on their own, for example, when frustrated doing homework or before a test.

Motivators involving silent thought

- *Rainbow Riding:* Students sit at desks, heads on the desks and eyes closed. Direct students to relax and think of your voice as you take them somewhere special. Allow about 15 seconds of silence; then, invite them to visualize the most beautiful rainbow ever, seeing all the colors, the huge arc, and the glistening ends where the rainbow dips down. Tell them to imagine they are sitting at the top of the rainbow and when you give the cue, they will slide down the arc. It will be a slow, gentle slide and they are to pay attention to everything they see and feel. Tell them you will let them know when they reach the bottom. Give the start cue and talk them through the "ride," making it last as long as possible (probably 30 seconds). Tell them to pay attention to what they land on and then to stay there until you give the return-to-me cue. Let students remain there for up to two minutes.

Follow-up: Students can discuss or write about what they saw, felt, smelled, or landed on.

- *Wandering Water:* From the silently seated positions, or from lying prone on the floor adjacent to desks, students close their eyes and listen to the silence for about 30 seconds. Tell them to listen as it starts to rain. Quietly describe the gentle dripping in any way desired, talking them through the rain becoming harder but still pleasant and refreshing. Then talk about hearing either a waterfall or ocean waves — big, thundering, splashing, and roaring. Return from the waves to the gentle rain, getting less until it stops. Students listen to the silence once again.

Follow-up: Discuss the sounds of moving water and where we find this in everyday life (e.g., fountains, music that simulates moving water). Talk about

Any of these motivators can be done to music if desired. I usually use gentle yoga-type music, such as that of George Zamphir; Tai Chi music; or sounds of nature. I love using these activities right after a very active class, such as physical education or art.

Good Idea

If you can afford to purchase a small indoor water fountain (often seen in massage parlors), keep it in your room and turn it on to help students "hear" water. Soothing on their own, the fountains are an excellent addition to "Wandering Water." A Grade 2 teacher colleague, given one by the family of one of her students, reported it had an amazing calming effect on her class.

why these sounds are so relaxing and what other sounds might have similar effects.

- *Autumn Leaves:* From silently seated positions or from lying prone on the floor adjacent to desks, students close their eyes and listen to the silence for about 30 seconds. Tell them they are going for a barefoot walk through autumn leaves. Via mind pictures they are to put themselves in a beautiful forest where all the trees are partially bare and the remaining leaves are falling down gently. Under their feet, dry leaves crunch as they walk and the autumn sun warms them from above. They are to listen carefully, breathe deeply, and feel the calm beauty of an autumn day. They meander through the woods on a trail until you tell them to return.

    Follow-up: Discuss how the walk made them feel or encourage them to journal their thoughts and feelings.

- *My Mantra:* By teaching students how to create and use a mantra — an expression or idea that is repeated and closely associated with, in this case, a sense of peace — teachers are giving them a lifelong technique for dealing with difficult situations. Begin by helping students create a personal mantra. The following steps may be useful.

    1. Think of a couple of words that express what you want to happen (e.g., "having strength, courage").
    2. Pick the strongest word and add the personal pronoun "I." ("I . . . courage.")
    3. Add a connecting word or any other word(s) that you feel will make your mantra work for you. Remember: Keep your mantra short and simple. ("I have courage.")
    4. Now, repeat your mantra several times in your mind.

Point out that students may have several mantras. No rule says that they must be restricted to one; however, most people find they keep returning to the same mantra. If students can't create one, offer them a choice of one of the following, or help them come up with one similar to any of the following.

I believe in me.	I am at peace.
I am okay.	I am relaxed.
I can do this on my own.	

Once mantras have been "found," at any time when the class needs a bit of peace, simply tell students to find a comfortable position, close their eyes, and silently repeat their mantras until you give the return-to-me cue. A colleague told me she used this technique with her Grade 3 students while on a field trip bus. They were excited and rowdy and getting louder by the minute. She cued for attention and used My Mantra. She said it worked so well the bus driver said he planned to create a mantra for himself.

    Follow-up: Discuss where and when using a mantra might be helpful. Invite students to write personal mantras in journals, perhaps with a few words explaining why they are personal.

- *Toes & Nose:* Once students have been instructed in how to use Toes & Nose, all they will need is the quick command "Toes & Nose" to immediately attempt to perform the almost impossible task. The idea is to wiggle the toes (inside the shoes), while wiggling the nose. Since they aren't allowed to wiggle noses with their fingers, usually what happens is that mouths, chins, eyebrows, and faces wiggle instead. This is unimportant. What is important is the silent pursuit of the action which serves to calm and relax and offer an instant change of pace. Perhaps some students can wiggle their noses; you may wish to use them as examples. But reinforce that this is not a contest, but a self-relaxation procedure that they can use for the rest of their lives. (Note it works wonderfully well for adults too.)

Follow-up: Discuss why something as seemingly silly as Toes & Nose can help reduce stress — stops the mind mutter, forces focus on something else — and invite ideas for other stress-reducing instant activities.

Teaching While in the Midst of Grief

Many of the motivators suggested in the preceding section serve to reduce stress in students. Do they reduce teacher stress, too? And what about teachers' personal pain and grief? Unfortunately, there are no quick motivators to help deal with these real and difficult matters, but a few suggestions may be helpful.

Everyone deals with tragedy; everyone experiences grief. Teachers are no different from anyone else in this regard; however, they differ greatly when it comes to the time of grieving. The nature of their profession makes it such that they have to time-slot their feelings and reactions so that they occur only between the hours of 4 p.m. and 7 a.m. During the other hours, when they face their students, they must be consummate actors who present the proverbial "teacher face."

I cannot think of another profession that carries this terrible load. Naturally, like everyone else, teachers go through the seven stages of grief: (1) shock and denial, (2) pain and guilt, (3) anger and bargaining, (4) depression and loneliness, (5) initial adjustment, (6) working through, and (7) acceptance and hope. Like others, they don't necessarily go through them in sequence or without considerable difficulty. But this is not what this section of *Teaching in Troubled Times* is about; it is about ways that these teachers, still grieving, can face their students, their teaching responsibilities, and their colleagues effectively.

I was fortunate to know Mrs. Wilkes, an exemplary teacher and my role model. When her husband of more than 40 years passed away, I wondered how she would ever face her rowdy Grade 3 class. She did as I should have guessed. She took a single day off work, then returned, smiling at all of us and forgiving us our uncomfortable attempts to comfort her. Her classroom was adjacent to mine; it was not unusual to watch her enter the room. She took a few moments to compose herself before opening her classroom door, smiled, and then went in. Her students knew of her loss, but not by anything Mrs. Wilkes did or didn't do.

They say a good teacher is like a candle; she consumes herself to light the way for others. That was Mrs. Wilkes. She never faltered. Her candle never flickered. I know she grieved, but at school, she always burned brightly.

When I asked my colleague how she managed her grief, she said, "My dear, I embrace my deep grief for Harold 12 hours a day and all days Saturday and Sunday when I'm not at church. The other time, at school, I am a teacher." As simple as that sounds, there is great truth therein. At another time, she told a different colleague who had also inquired as to her uncanny ability to put on her "teacher face": "I weep for my Harold when the time is right. The rest of the time, work, I've found, is the best antidote."

As another illustration, a male teacher, Dave Androchuck (Mr. A to his Grade 6 class), experienced the devastating loss of his three-year-old son. When he returned to work following the school board–allotted time for grieving, we were all worried about how he would manage his classroom, especially since his wife had called and warned us that Dave was not himself, that he was "very angry."

At the time I was the school counselor so it fell to me to welcome Dave back and keep a caring eye on him. His wife hadn't exaggerated. Dave was an angry man. His temper flared at the slightest provocation. He snapped at secretaries and colleagues alike such that we all tiptoed around him or avoided him. He came into the staff room only to bang cups around and grumble at the fridge. The principal asked me to find out how Dave was in the classroom, since out of the class he was a complete bear. In response to gentle questions to his students I heard, "Mr. A is just the same old Mr. A" and "He's cool, man. You'd never know he was hurtin'." I was pleasantly surprised. And when I found reasons to visit Dave's room spontaneously, the class was always focused, the mood was warm and comfortable, and Dave, himself, looked and acted just like the old Dave.

Finally, I approached Dave after school and asked how he was managing, tentatively pointing out the huge difference between his in-class and out-of-class behavior. He confided that he "hurt like hell" and that he felt like a live volcano was inside his gut, but he had figured out how to "switch it off" when with his students. He apologized for being unable to switch it off with colleagues too, but said he had only enough energy to maintain that facade in the classroom. I applauded his incredible efforts. His "teacher face" was a feat of pure determination, and I knew then that all teachers could summon "necessary magic" if they had to.

During much reflection on this expectation that teachers will be someone completely different in the classroom than out of it, especially when consumed with grief, I wondered whether their inner pain surfaced in any sneaky, insidious ways. I quite recently found out that it did. I lost my best friend, a little dog that I believed was my only true soul mate. If you have ever lost a pet, you will understand my grief. It was so much worse than I could have imagined. But I had learned from Mrs. Wilkes that work helps one to deal with the pain of loss, so I began writing. After 4 or 5 pages, I printed the hard copy, which is how I proof my own work. I was astonished to find that my text was total nonsense. It made no sense; it read like an essay written by a Grade 3 student who was trying to write like an adult but did not understand semantics, pragmatics, or syntax.

This was an eye-opener for me.

Apparently, grief does something nasty to cognition, at least as far as writing is concerned. I did some research. I found this observation by Ralph Waldo Emerson: "Sorrow makes us all children again — destroys all differences of intellect. The wisest know nothing."

The other huge awareness that came with the loss of my pet was that I could, and did, feel happy again. I was sure I would never smile again until a friend confided that she, too, felt the same way when grieving and that eventually, she did smile with her heart once more.

Teachers, then, may well have to deal with grief a bit differently than other people, and in today's troubled world with its new pressures, demands, restraints, and faults they, like everyone else, tend to suffer much grief. Perhaps they need a little help or even just the reassurance that what they are doing is okay.

Although most of us are familiar with the symptoms of grief, I have compiled the ideas that appear at the top of page 104 from a number of sources so that teachers can recognize the physical and mental symptoms of grief not only in themselves, but also in their students:

- restlessness, distraction
- inability to sleep
- cognitive impairment
- disturbance in appetite
- tendency to tire easily or feel unnaturally fatigued
- feelings of anger or guilt
- not wanting to see friends
- not finding enjoyment in usually pleasurable pursuits
- feelings of loss not just for a person or pet, but for all the activities associated with that person or pet
- anxiety, even to the point of panic attacks
- loneliness, even when surrounded by others
- helplessness, a sense of never being able to feel happy again

Dealing effectively with grief while maintaining a full teaching load

Like Mrs. Wilkes or Dave, teachers experiencing grief are expected to keep teaching and to be filled with passion, enthusiasm, and joy. Like Mrs. Wilkes and Dave, they daily put on their "teacher faces" and face their classrooms with no hint of inner pain. And unfortunately, today, there appear to be more grieving teachers "still at work" than ever before. (When I was a child, a teacher who had lost a parent was away for six months of the term — that would not happen today.)

The death of a loved one is not the only source of grief. Other sources include job loss, divorce or separation, illness, catastrophe, economic disaster, and even a loss of freedom (e.g., loss of an automobile). If these sound a lot like the disasters noted in Chapter 1, it's because they are the same troubles that in today's world are brought to the fore. The result? Many more people, teachers among them, are grieving. I hope that the following suggestions will provide help.

- Allow yourself to grieve, but set boundaries, such as not during school hours.
- Don't try to rush the process. Grief can take a long time, and for some, it may never really disappear. Do not ignore the pain as this will only make it worse in the long run, but assign a time each day when you will set your grief aside.
- Become a master at using the "teacher face."
- Ask colleagues not to talk to you about the loss at this time. Grief is manageable until someone tries to be comforting.
- Avoid thinking of everything in terms of the person who has gone: "___ would have loved that." If you catch yourself doing that, use the Stop-Think technique. Tell yourself to stop thinking about that now and allow yourself to think about it later. "Later" might be in the car on the way home or not at all.
- When not within the grief-free time boundaries of school hours, allow yourself to cry, if that is how you feel, and grieve deeply. The notion that it is important to be strong in the face of loss is a myth. Do whatever you need to do to grieve.
- Schedule activities that allow and encourage you to vent and expel negative energy. Dave took up racquet ball, something he had never done and later admitted was never good at. Or, get completely involved with the physical education class. If the kids are playing indoor soccer, play along with them.
- Take a break from cognitive pursuits such as evening marking and planning. The brain doesn't function well during grieving. You will still be able to teach, but avoid anything that is not completely necessary, at least for a while. Extra-

Good Idea
Borrow U.S. President Obama's phrase "Yes, we can," and change it to "Yes, I can," and make that your mantra. Say it repeatedly until you feel your "teacher face" is securely in place.

"When you are sorrowful look again in your heart, and you shall see that in truth you are weeping for that which has been your delight."
— Kahlil Gibran

"Don't cry because it's over. Smile because it happened."
— Dr. Seuss

curricular sports activities, on the other hand, may be therapeutic. Try them before you make a firm commitment.

- Lean on others — colleagues, friends, and family — and accept assistance. Remember that others may want to help you but don't know how. Make suggestions. For example, ask a peer to take your noon supervision so that you will have a few quiet moments to recharge.

- Talk about your loss when you can. If possible, do not grieve alone; however, avoid sharing grief with your students even if they question you. They may be filled with compassion and love, but they are still young and saddling them with such a huge burden is unfair.

- Give yourself time. You will smile again, not just the teacher-face smile but a total, from-the-gut-I-feel-it smile. Sometimes just knowing this, just believing that eventually you will feel better, is therapeutic. I know it was for me.

As a final word about teachers' grief, I share the following comment from a Grade 7 student. The boy witnessed a teacher from his school crying in her car after dismissal. He confided that he had been upset by what he had seen because he "didn't think teachers ever cried unless it was because kids were mean to them." I assured him that teachers did indeed cry and were full of all the same fears and worries as every other human.

Letting Go: Sending Precious Students into an Uncertain Future

"Of course, I can let my kids go. No problem," a first-year teacher told me as she watched her very first students leaving at the end of June, tears rolling down her cheeks. We laughed together, but it may not be a laughing matter. Teachers get attached to their students, some more than others. It's human nature. The more caring and compassionate a teacher is, the more attached she may become.

Letting go can be a real problem. A Grade 6 teacher told me in June 2009 that more than ever she hated to see her students leave. "Life is so nasty right now," she explained, "what with all the wars and disease and all." (The H1N1 pandemic scare was just starting.) "I worry that I haven't given them enough, haven't prepared them to face, well, just about anything. It used to be easier . . ." I considered seriously her words and realized that she was probably expressing a common concern of today's teachers. How do they know if their students have learned enough, matured enough, taken enough with them to survive in a chaotic world? The answer is simple but unsatisfying — they don't know! Yet they are expected to say good-bye at the end of a school year.

It's more than the letting go in June, however. The problem exists throughout the year, and along with today's many worldwide troubles, its prevalence seems to have increased. It may be that the more horrible and chaotic our world becomes, the more teachers who care become mother hens who want to shield and protect their young: the problem with teachers "rescuing," "saving," "defending," and "over-assisting" also seems to be on the rise. It may be that the current curriculum demands are so exhausting that teachers feel sorry for little people who are expected to cram their minds far too quickly and far too full. It may be that over-burdened teachers can't keep up with expectations and feel the need to do things themselves "because it's faster" rather than allow children the time required to complete a task. Whatever the reason, there exists a problem with some teachers "letting go." (And certainly I plead guilty.) I'm sure all teachers know exactly what

I offer these suggestions as hints for improved teacher performance, based on personal experience and experience observing colleagues. Depending on the students, they will work *some of the time*.

I'm talking about. Here are a few suggestions that may help to remedy, or at least clarify, this sticky situation.

- Resist the temptation to *always* read stories and passages out loud in a shared reading approach (where each student sees some form of the text, such as a separate book, photocopied page, flip chart, text on overhead, or PowerPoint). Shared reading ensures that everyone "gets the message," but it may not reinforce the importance of students reading on their own — in real life, there isn't always someone to read aloud. Sometimes, students become complacent and want to "follow along" rather than read independently. An alternative is to read the first part of a text and then have students finish it independently. Naturally, reading aloud is good — and very important — so don't ignore it completely. Just remember that kids can read alone if the expectation to do so is there.

- Be careful during a test or exam not to give too much help. I appreciate that we all want our students to do well, but if we end up "doing the questions for them" not only are results jeopardized, but so is their self-confidence. (*Teacher thinks I can't do this.*) Remember, kids will use whatever help you are willing to give, whether they need it or not.

- Allow and accept mistakes. Point out how mistakes are chances to learn and grow. Some teachers find it hard not to jump in and help students when they are headed towards mistakes, but by constantly doing this, they send out the message that they lack confidence in the children. Mistakes are okay, good even. Use them to teach and help children to learn from them. Remember, by "saving" kids too often, we risk impeding their growth and development.

- Respect students as equals, not below or above you or their peers. Respect their individual idiosyncrasies and support their weaknesses as well as their strengths. In other words, remember that they are little people with all the same fears and doubts as adults.

- Always reinforce any steps students take towards independence (e.g., the first time a child attempts a previously ignored task alone). When kids problem-solve on their own, they take a huge step towards self-sufficiency; be sure to tell them how proud you are of their "independent behaviors." Using the word "independent" frequently shows the degree of importance you give it and raises students' awareness of being independent. Remember, life for students exists outside teacher control.

- Be alert to the possible creation of co-dependency between you and any of the students. Although rare, this can happen when the teacher unconsciously does too much for a student or makes excuses for him to the point where the student becomes dependent and unable to move ahead without teacher support. You can't take the students home with you; eventually, they need to stand alone.

Remember that in teaching, we can rarely, if ever see the end results. What we do today will reflect in our students' future. Our profession doesn't provide for many spontaneous reinforcements, if we are seeking those in lifelong skills we hope to have taught. For the most part, immediate gratification is rare. This may be part of the reason some of us have a tough time "letting go." Like parents, we, too, want to protect our children from the world and its troubles. We want to shelter and shield and watch over and witness the success of our teaching. But we can't. The best teachers let go with smiles and joyful "teacher faces" and then turn attention to the next wide-eyed students waiting to be enthralled.

The Curriculum Conundrum

As if not enough that we live in a troubled time, teachers have to deal with elaborate, difficult, and time-consuming curriculum as well. The world is racing ahead with breakneck speed, and students are expected to keep up. Do you remember the days of the 3 Rs or, further back, the one-room schoolhouse where everyone arrived at school weeks late because they had helped with harvesting? Today we try to cram so much into the heads of our students that no wonder both teachers and students often succumb to the load. Concerned teachers can make subtle changes to alleviate this burden.

As far as curriculum is concerned, teachers need to remind themselves constantly that *not all that is in the curriculum must be covered*. In fact, doing so would be impossible. They must be picky. They must figure out what their students need to be successful, to grow, to get along happily in life, and teach that. For instance, do all students need to memorize all the dates of the many events studied in history? What about the ones who are going to be laborers? Or retail salesclerks? Is this something that could be learned later on a need-to-know basis?

Let's be realistic. Let's teach what is useful right now — today. We live in a world ridden with risks, fears, insecurities, catastrophes, anxieties, and unhappiness, and our students are not exempt from these troubles. These twenty-first century students need to be prepared, by today's teachers, to live in an uncertain future. How can modern teachers make the best decisions about what to teach and what to ignore?

Teachers, you do need to familiarize yourselves with the curriculum mandates, but don't worry if covering them becomes impossible. Once you know your students and appreciate their abilities and needs, certain curriculum content will seem superfluous; allow it to be so. Remember that in your classroom, you are in charge, and the most important thing you can teach your students is how to learn independently. If they are independent learners, it will help them advance into the new decade with confidence and, it is hoped, with fewer fears and anxieties than were experienced in the last one. The following suggestions speak to that end:

- Teach students through modeling and through specific lessons on cooperation, networking, and socialization to cultivate an interest in others. In doing so, you show them how to live more happily.
- Encourage them to make habits of positive actions (e.g., completing homework on time). Excellence is a habit.
- Help each student to figure out his or her individual gifts as this is part of the journey to enlightenment. Provide specific positive reinforcement when you notice a strength, perhaps a skill in movement or dance; or, have students identify and list personal areas of strength and then confirm those with which you most agree.
- Remind students of what they are capable by adding little notes to their work, for example, "You are very good at creative writing." You can also do this during one-on-one conferences and can constantly encourage them in areas where you know they can do better.

Recharging Teachers' Batteries in Times of Tough Teaching

Teacher burnout!

The term *teacher burnout* has become a buzz word. Everyone tosses it around, and all teachers experience it to some degree during their professional lives. Meanwhile, society tends to think that teacher burnout is an excuse, an explanation for poor performance or for requiring time off.

I think the word is all wrong — *burned out* implies nothing left, all ashes and dust, no more spark or even a glowing ember. I will not use that term in this book — I choose to think of it as a forbidden term. Instead, I have chosen to refer to this very real state experienced by all teachers at some times as the time of "battery recharging." Some batteries have a shelf life and are dead before they ever begin. Some batteries can't handle tough or prolonged use and die a slow death, gradually losing power. Some batteries are rechargeable — like teachers. When teachers are faced with the inevitable feeling of low batteries, when they are worn out, tired, frustrated, and unexcited by anything, then they need to recharge. So here it goes: no *teacher burnout*. That's the last time I will use that distasteful term.

This section will deal with positive ways to recharge teachers with positive energy. Too many positives? Not really. Maintaining that positivity is what prevents teacher "low battery warnings."

All modern teachers are familiar with the common suggestions for dealing with low batteries. Much information has been written about and for this problem. Indeed, that wealth of information may be part of the problem. When a teacher is already experiencing the effects of a low battery, the mere thought of seeking through realms of material for that one nugget that might help could well be too much. Besides, we have all heard it before. So, *Teaching in Troubled Times* offers a few different ideas: ways to counter the negative effects of a low battery before it gives out completely, ways to *recharge* teachers' batteries. These largely original ideas have worked for my colleagues and most certainly for me. Use any or all or none at all. They appear in no particular sequence. All have been, and are being, used successfully today.

Sometimes just reading about an issue is enough to provide a modicum of relief from it. For instance, if a teacher — you — reads the following suggestions and says, "What is she talking about? I don't need this!" then chances are you feel a little better already. Good. You have already recharged your battery a bit. The key is — don't procrastinate all you overworked and stressed-out teachers. Use them now!

An interesting article in *The Edmonton Journal* spoke of our current not-so-good tendency to postpone pleasures. I think teachers are masters at this; we constantly tell ourselves lies, such as we will "have fun when the marking is done," "go to the movies after interviews," or "go for a long walk on the weekend." The rule here, and it *is* a rule, is *Do not postpone pleasures,* especially if your batteries are fading. Invest a little time now to have a much more positive time later. Remember that everything you say and do makes a difference, so maintaining the health and vibrancy of your inner battery is mandatory. Think "a spoonful of happiness today equals a wheelbarrow of joy tomorrow." I hope that at least one of the following strategies will be a spoonful of happiness for you.

- *Buddy Bonus:* This involves two people, so involve a colleague with whom you have a good relationship. On a preset date (e.g., last teaching Friday in each month), you will give each other a surprise bonus. First, a price is established

Let me assure you that this simple activity has huge benefits. It's always so much fun to get a "surprise." It's equally fun to find a surprise for another person. On one occasion, my buddy and I had the same thoughts. It was June and we, like all teachers in June, were exhausted. On the morning of Buddy Bonus day we accidentally met in the hall on our way to each other's classes, each with a bottle of wine. We laughed for a long time about that.

($15 maximum is good) and during the month, each buddy seeks a little something for the other person. *The seeking does not have to take a lot of time.* There are so many interesting little gifts to choose from, including candy, small veggie tray, flowers, plant, seasonal trinkets, such as a Christmas ornament, bunch of pens or pencils, teachers' magazine, movie pass, homemade cookies — the list is limited only by your imagination.

A great adaptation of Buddy Bonus is to involve the whole school staff, including teachers, custodians, and aides (or as many as are interested). Draw names randomly and follow the same procedure. The activity is sort of a "Secret Santa" that goes on all year. What fun!

How does Buddy Bonus recharge batteries? Getting a little surprise, even when you expect it, is a joyful experience. It is something to look forward to, and it generally evokes a smile. One of the best ways to recharge a human battery is to ply it with smiles. Try it and see.

- *Clean-a-Closet:* A colleague uses this tactic every time she starts to feel her batteries running low. She literally cleans a closet (or a cupboard, or drawers — any small, confined space). She convinced me that the mindless nature of this activity always gives her batteries a boost and that she feels better afterward. Needless to say, she has the cleanest closets and cupboard I have ever seen. When I asked her how she found time to do this, her response was that when she is "near breaking" (her words) she is usually too distractible and restless, or too lethargic and depressed, to do anything constructive related to teaching anyway; she sets a timer (usually no more than 30 minutes) and proceeds to clean a closet. When I asked what happened if the timer went off and she wasn't finished the cleaning (I had visions of a pile of clothes on the closet floor), she said, "I just shut the door and wait until the next time I feel like that. I know it won't be long. I *am* a teacher after all."

How does Clean-a-Closet recharge batteries? It is sort of like meditation. It gives the brain time to stop buzzing.

My ideal location for a silent sojourn has always been outside on my deck, weather permitting, when the early morning calm was all pervasive.

- *Early Silent Sojourn:* This is my favorite anti-battery-death activity. No matter how busy you are, even if you have children and husband to get off every morning, you can make time for a 10 to 15 minute silent sojourn. In this brief time just for you, you can sit in silence with a cup of tea or coffee, the newspaper, a book, or just with your thoughts *before* everyone else gets up. Be conscious of your breathing — deep and slow — and of your body being completely without tension.

I know that many of you will say you don't have time for this, you have too much to do and if you could get up 15 minutes earlier you would use that time to mark or plan or . . . I say, please *please* make the time. Just try this a few times and you will understand why it is so important. Tell your family ahead of time what you are doing and explain that they are not to interrupt you.

How does Early Silent Sojourn recharge batteries? It starts the day on a gentle note, with a positive push towards all that awaits you. It encourages breathing and a few precious minutes of complete relaxation. When the day gets tough, remind yourself that tomorrow you will have another Early Silent Sojourn.

- *Guard Dog:* A common reason for battery failure in teachers is simply overwork; they try to do it all. I appreciate that at-home work is necessary. There are always marking and planning, and no time for this at school. However, all batteries get weak and will die if not recharged, and sitting for too long a period at home doing at-school work is a surefire way to kill a perfectly good battery. So, here's my suggestion. Adopt a guard dog — not a real dog, but a real person (usually a significant other but perhaps a child) — whose responsibility is to enforce the Stop Working Now rule. You know what happens. You start marking (planning, reviewing, creating) and tell yourself you'll stop in an hour, but the hours zip past, you begin to slump, your head starts to ache, your eyes feel as if they have sand in them, and before you know it, it's midnight. When you finally stand up, every muscle hurts. Carrying out marathon marking schedules is one of the most harmful activities in which teachers are involved. So, delegate a guard dog to come and remove you (physically, if necessary) from your post when a reasonable time has passed.

Guard Dog was originally my husband's idea. He would come after an hour had passed and pull me away for "a cup of tea" or "to watch this on TV." It's a brilliant idea. If, after your guard dog has interrupted and moved you away from your desk, you still feel the need to work longer, set another time, and tell the guard dog when to stop you again. In most instances, after the first reminder you'll realize it is better for all if you cease and desist at that time.

How does having a guard dog help recharge batteries? It prevents total power drain by forcing a change of venue, and possibly even adding years of life to your skeleton. In addition, it shares a bit of the burden of your after-hours work with someone else. Any sharing lightens a load. One teacher confided that her husband said he never realized how hard she worked until he assumed the guard dog role and had to pry her away from endless marking.

- *Borrowed "Bud"*: Everyone knows the importance of walking, but I have included it here because in my experience, teachers, the same ones who diligently teach their students that walking is a valid form of exercise, are the worst at not walking. It's the same old story: "I don't have time." I apologize for the cliché, but you don't have time *not* to walk. I won't go into the many, many benefits of walking, but I will make a suggestion that might be the impetus for you to walk regularly. Borrow a "bud": a neighbor's dog. I'm assuming you do not have a dog of your own because if you do, the walking issue would be moot. Dogs *insist* on going for walks and if you are not doing this with your pet, well, you're truly missing out. So, find a neighbor's dog you like (every neighborhood has dogs these days, and many of them never get walked). Make a deal to walk the dog once a week on a certain day or night at a specific time. You have now made a commitment. You are a responsible person with integrity so you must honor that obligation. Good for you. Now, you'll be gaining the pleasurable benefits of walking and will have a buddy to share it with you.

How does borrowing a "bud" recharge batteries? Walking reduces stress, clears the mind, opens the soul, regulates both heart and breathing, and generally promotes a sense of wellness. Finally, walking with a dog is just plain fun. On a playful side, I recall a male teacher who, when I said we were going to try the "borrowed bud" idea, promptly announced happily, "Great! Bud is my favorite beer!"

- *Morning E-mail Group (ME group)*: E-mails drive us all crazy, especially when they load up our desk computers at school. This suggestion, however, looks at these techie-notes in a more positive light. It involves five or more people, not necessarily just other teachers, connected by e-mail. Each person is responsible for a specific workday. If more than five people are involved, work out some sort of regular system whereby everyone gets a turn in sequence. The responsible person must send the group a funny or positive e-mail the evening prior to his specific day (e.g., if responsible for Tuesdays, the e-mail goes out Monday night or late afternoon). These tidbits must be short and sassy. (No one likes to plod through those video feeds that seem to take ages when busy.) The idea is that each member of the ME group will have an early morning "positive" e-mail to enjoy. This activity need not be time consuming, either for sender or receivers.

Messages can take a variety of forms:

a quotation ("Joy is the feeling of grinning inside.")
a joke (e.g., The teacher asked, "Can you give me a good example of how heat expands things and cold contracts them?" "Well," one alert student answered, "the days are much longer in summer.")
a good idea (e.g., For a juicer hamburger, add cold water to the beef before grilling — 1/2 cup to 1 pound of meat)
a word of advice (e.g., Give people a second chance because no one is perfect. Love all that you can, give all that you have, smile away your days, and dream away your nights.)
a bit of trivia (e.g., What is Charlie Brown's teacher known for saying? *Wah wah wah wah.*)

How does the ME group help recharge batteries? It starts each day on a positive note, perhaps with a smile, and at least with the awareness that someone is out there, thinking of you. It promotes an important sense of connection.

- *Head Massage:* Now don't ignore this suggestion because it sounds silly — it really works! We are all aware of the benefits both physical and emotional from massage. Planning and going for a massage are time consuming, not to mention rather costly, and for these reasons teachers seldom take advantage of this excellent way to recharge their batteries. So, I'm suggesting an equally effective alternative: a head massage. The best head massages are provided by professional masseurs, but here again the time and money elements come into play (note, though, that a head massage takes less time than a full-body massage and can be fitted into a lunch hour). A good alternative is to share head massages with a colleague or significant other. They are simple to give and reap huge benefits. Here are brief steps. More detailed steps can be found online by using the keywords "head massage."

  1. Start at the shoulders and gently rub in towards the neck in small circles. Repeat with more pressure.
  2. Hands on shoulders, make small thumb circles on either side of neck, moving up to the hair line.
  3. Stand behind, hands on each side of head, move in small circles (like shampooing), gradually moving up to crown. Make contact with fingers and palm of hand. Repeat several times.
  4. With fingers on forehead, make small circles while moving up and back.
  5. Make small, light circles at temples.
  6. Apply gentle pressure with fingers to eyebrows and hold for 15 seconds.
  7. Lightly stroke fingers from brow back over head to neck, repeating for 60 seconds.

How does Head Massage help to recharge batteries? It relieves stress by stimulating circulation and addressing both physical and mental tension. It can relieve headaches and back tension.

- *User-Friendly Volunteer(s):* I completely understand that volunteers, helpful though they may be, sometimes cause more work and hassle for you, so, here's an idea for user-friendly volunteers. Begin by collecting names of volunteers. Take a bit of time to canvass, call homes, send letters, and visit seniors' centres or community leagues. The time taken to gather a group of volunteers is well worth it.

  Next, call a meeting of them all, a friendly, get-to-know-you event with one key objective: to elect or encourage a volunteer president. The president will be responsible for organizing all the other volunteers, and this is where you begin to enjoy the real value of volunteer assistance. If you are lucky enough to have a good president (and your enthusiasm will ensure this), this person will be the only one you will need to be involved with. It will become her responsibility to obtain lists from you of what you want done and when it needs to be done, then to assign it to volunteers. Work will include arranging helpers for in and out of class, for field trips, for photocopying, for "grunt" work (e.g., cupboard cleaning), and for helping individual students — basically, for anything you might need help with. The advantage to this system— what makes it really user friendly — is that the president will get to know the strengths, weaknesses, schedules, likes, interests, and so on of the other volunteers, and so will use them effectively and efficiently. Once you get this system going, all you'll need to do is prepare a weekly list for the president. Of course you can contact her during the week too, and she will know just who will be free to help.

  This User-Friendly Volunteer plan sounds like a lot of work and initially takes a bit of effort, but it works so smoothly you will wonder why you haven't used it before. The trick is, of course, to find a good president who will work pro bono for personal satisfaction. Even this isn't as difficult as it sounds; many stay-at-home parents are delighted with this responsibility.

  User-Friendly Volunteers is an excellent program for several classes working together or even for an entire school. There can be an honorarium for a president if a whole school is involved; coordinating volunteers becomes quite a large undertaking, but once a president understand the role, the program runs smoothly and is truly the basis of user-friendly volunteers.

- *AA — Alternate Adult(s):* Teacher-talk is good: it is a necessary part of staff-room behavior and is often an information-sharing practice. When your battery is running low, however, and you feel susceptible to dead-battery syndrome, it's time for AA, for the "alternate adult," one or more adults who are *not* educators but with whom you can carry on a conversation, attend some form of entertainment, accompany to a sporting event, or play a sport — basically, do something away from all evidence of school and teaching. You'll know when you need this diversion; consider it your "AA" (Alternate Adult) support group, and refuse to say a word about teaching for the entire time in their company.

  If an AA slips and asks you how your day went, frown, remind your friend that that topic is taboo, then smile and change the subject. This conscious temporary forgetting about the stress of the occupation is extremely healthy. Once your AA becomes used to the role (you can make a bit of a joke about it), he or she may even call you to see if you need some AA or ask for some AA, too. In that case, be available.

- *The "Me Letter":* Write yourself a letter (Dear Me) in which you whine, complain, condemn, blame, chastise, shout out your anger . . . whatever. Date it

Once, my president was a young pregnant woman who was unemployed at the time and eager to get involved with the local school. We met while I was canvassing the neighborhood for volunteers in September, and she remained for the entire term, even managing volunteers with a new baby at home.

and sign it. Use as many awful words as you want to; no one is going to read the letter but you. As quickly as possible, get all your emotions out on paper, then put the missive in a sealed envelope and mail it to yourself. When you get it back and reread it, one of two things will probably happen: you'll laugh, which will mean you are feeling better already, or you'll get angry or upset again and think that the words "don't even begin" to express your frustration. In the latter case, do it all over again. Remember to keep the letters and eventually, one that makes you laugh will arrive. The "Me Letter" is a very effective method of dealing with personal anxiety.

- *The Half-Full Coffee Cup:* We are all tired, I am sure, of hearing the "glass half full/empty" statement, but in this case, it applies. I will however alter it to make it more appropriate to teacher-battery recharging. For all teachers, it is now a coffee cup — the one that usually sits on your desk, half-filled with cold coffee. When you need to recharge, immediately consider how often or to what degree you dwell on the negative — that is, the half-empty coffee cup of too many students, not enough time, too few books, uncooperative parents, too many meetings, a ridiculous curriculum — and STOP. Make yourself stop dwelling on how bad the situation is or how awful you feel — this is called "thought shifting," and anyone can do it. If you want to end up with a dead battery that will no longer take a charge, then stay negative, but if you would like to charge up and get moving again, foster positivity. Here are a few suggestions to help you do just that.

Formula Five: Fostering Positivity

Thought-shift. Use thought shifting by telling yourself to *stop* the flow of thoughts, then focusing on anything entirely different (e.g., an amusing movie you recently saw or all the leaves that have fallen in your yard). By stopping the negative flow, you'll be giving yourself permission to think positively. When you want to employ this tactic, imagine a big, red STOP sign in your face.

Surround yourself with positive people. If some colleagues tend to be "whiners," avoid them and hang out with the others. In the evenings, if your significant other is being less than positive, remove yourself from the room, and phone or e-mail a positive person immediately.

Make positive affirmations. Repeat a positive affirmation over and over to yourself. *I am not upset by any of this. I am smiling inside. I am confident and powerful.* It's hard to be negative when you are telling yourself how good you are.

Be grateful. Specifically think of something you are grateful for (e.g., your pet, your home, your health). It's hard to be upset and grateful at the same time. Positivity aligns itself with gratefulness.

Think opposites. First, use the STOP tactic and then consciously think of an opposite to whatever is disturbing you the most. For example, "not enough books for all the students" could be matched by *I don't have to teach that ___ today and we can read instead.* "Never enough time to finish the curriculum" could be addressed by *I can pick only what the kids will need and like.*

- *The Potlatch Hour:* This idea is borrowed loosely from the Northern Pacific Coast First Nations practice of giving away items that were meaningful to them. In this case, however, it refers to giving away a single hour of your

Thought-shift.
Surround yourself with positive people
Make positive affirmations.
Be grateful.
Think opposites.

Brainstorming Opposites
Sometimes, it's hard to find an opposite, but it should always be possible. For instance, when a friend lost her job and was about to lose her home also, she implored me to find a positive opposite. She was angry, depressed, and extremely negative about everything. I failed to help her, but within a few days, she called to tell me she had found a positive opposite. Her health had been troublesome (unknown to me) and now that she was unemployed, she was going to sell her home and do what she had always dreamed of doing: travel. She had spent an entire night brainstorming "opposites," and that was what she had arrived at.

time. Now before you sigh and comment that you don't have a single hour to spare, please finish reading about this wonderful, effective way to recharge a failing battery. If you are suffering from any degree of you-know-what, then you probably aren't using time well at present, and yes, you do have an hour a week to involve yourself in potlatch.

Simply volunteer for a single pre-designated hour a week at somewhere that is not a school with people who are not students. Commit to that hour (e.g., Saturday 11 a.m. to noon) with whomever or whatever interests you and reap the enormous benefits of giving your time. If you have never volunteered, you're in for a pleasant surprise. If you have volunteered before, you are already familiar with the advantages volunteering brings you. Volunteering is like the perfect meditation without having to learn how to meditate. It takes you completely away from your stresses, worries, and fears, and drops you into a completely different environment where you basically can do no wrong and are appreciated just for being there. What a perfect pat-on-the-back for someone whose battery is low.

I suggest volunteering at seniors' homes, perhaps reading the newspaper to visually impaired (which is usually most of them), talking to others, or playing cards or board games. This is the easiest and most rewarding volunteering as far as I'm concerned. But if this avenue doesn't appeal to you, check the local paper; agencies are crying for help, especially when so many service-type jobs have been cut. You could help at an animal shelter, a veterinary clinic, a hospital or hospice, or at a community centre. I can't emphasize enough the value of the potlatch hour for anyone in personal jeopardy — please don't discard this idea until you give it a try. And remember, once committed to that hour, it's your responsibility to be there. You won't regret it, I promise.

- *The Comfort List:* Not to be confused with a "bucket list," this is a list of activities or indulgences that provide you with instant gratification, with comfort. When your battery is flagging, it is usually quite impossible to think of anything that would make you feel better, so, now is the time to write that Comfort List. Write it, add to it at any time, store it safely, and let others know where it is and what it is so that if you are ever hitting that dangerously low battery, someone who cares may be able to help you with something on your list.

What goes on the list? Well, it's entirely personal and selfish, but items from mine include a half-hour of silence, sipping Pinot Noir; a Dairy Queen peanut buster parfait; a slow, solitary walk in the woods; the opportunity to read from *I Think I'm Having One of Those Decades* by Gordon Kirkland while drinking a venté vanilla latte at Starbucks; and a full hour alone in a Chapters bookstore. There are others, but you get the idea.

I am serious about your creating this list immediately; if you don't, you never will.

I share the following little story. While writing this book, I experienced a huge loss and accompanying "blank slate" brain. I found myself slipping to a nasty place. I was in my office, but my battery was dangerously low. My husband then appeared with a glass of Pinot Noir. He proceeded to turn off my computer and physically led me to the single comfortable, seldom-used chair beside my desk. "This is number 3 on your comfort list thing," he said, and left, taking the phone and shutting the door behind him. His intervention worked.

A final word about dead batteries: There is no magic pill for a dead battery; sometimes you have to exchange it for a new one. However, with the many ways to recharge a battery today, the trick is to "plug in" to one of them and allow yourself time to recharge well before your inner battery goes dead. Teachers — you know when you're slipping, when you're in need of help, when life is threatening to overwhelm you and defeat you, but you are often reluctant to admit it. Perhaps this is because you belong to one of the giving professions, one of the leading and supporting professions, one of the lean-on-me professions, and are therefore are disinclined to lean on others. Wrong, so wrong. Considering how much caring and energy are taken from you, absorbed from you, daily, you need to replenish yourself regularly. You need to understand your own limits, know your own boundaries, and recognize your own symptoms of depletion. Then, you must be sure to take action, perhaps try a few of the suggestions offered here, and ask for help.

Possible Answers to Today's Tough Questions

Today's teachers are faced with many tough questions, probably because students are faced with many tough situations and issues attributable at least in part to today's troubled times. Foremost in these troubled times are the current ongoing wars around the world. Often, it's difficult to come up with a good response right "on the spot." Often, in retrospect, we think "oh, why didn't I say . . . ," when at the time, with an eager face watching closely and expecting an answer, the response was less than adequate. Teachers know one thing for sure: they *must* answer. It's not good enough to say, "Ask your parents." I'm not suggesting that teachers tell their students *not* to ask or involve their parents, but to remember that there are good reasons to answer a student's questions immediately, with as much accuracy as you think wise at the moment. In their eyes the teacher is the knowledgeable one, the person who knows everything. If the teacher fails to answer, or answer nonchalantly or indifferently, there is the possibility the question will take on greater importance, raise a higher degree of unrest or fear, or become a silent anxiety for the child.

There are a few general rules for responding to tough or sensitive questions. Teachers need to ask themselves "How much does the child already know? Can I elaborate on that or will a brief answer do? How does the age of the child affect what I will say?" They can then respond with the following in mind.

- Answer in an honest and matter-of-fact manner, providing just enough information to satisfy the child. Avoid embellishing unless more questions are asked.
- Give children permission to talk about their feelings (e.g., "Are you worried about . . .?"). Always reassure the child that his feelings are normal. Put his feelings into words for him if possible: "You'd like it if your daddy came home . . ."
- Keep your own biases out of the responses, but do share your emotional reactions without burdening or going into great detail. You might say, "That frightens me too, but . . ."
- Remember that children will see you as a role model so be careful of not only what you say, but how you act. If you say you are not worried about something yet act worried, they will receive a mixed message that can be more harmful than no message at all.

• If you don't know how to respond, say, "That's an interesting question. I'll see what I can find out about it." Return to the student with information as soon as possible.

The following sample questions and responses are provided as guidelines. Since answers will differ according to the ages of the students, it's impossible to provide foolproof responses. These questions were shared with me by worried teachers, who wondered how to respond in the best manner. The suggested responses are a combination of their replies, my experience, and my research on the topic. I have shared these here to give some ideas for good responses and to help create a sense of connection among new-decade teachers. You are not alone. All teachers today are being asked these sorts of questions; all teachers today will have to quickly assess their own knowledge, their students' knowledge, and their personal stances on the queries. Sometimes, it helps to know how a colleague would handle the situation.

Question: What happens when something dies? (Asked after the death of Grade 2 class mascot)
Response: It's confusing to understand, but the person or animal stops breathing. They can't feel or see or hear anything any more, so that would be good if the person had been in pain. All living things die. When someone or something we love dies, we miss them and feel sad.

Question: Why do some people, like terrorists, have to hurt others? (From male Grade 3 student)
Response: I don't know why some people use violence to express themselves, but I do know that violence doesn't solve problems and everyone in (Canada) is working to keep us safe.

Question: Will there be a terrorist attack on us? How do we know if we're safe? I saw this guy on the bus who had a turban. Maybe he was a terrorist? (From a boy in Grade 5)
Response: We don't believe there will be an attack, but no one can ever know for sure. What I do know for sure is that the man in the turban was not a terrorist. Remember that we discussed how wearing a turban is just a sign of culture? I also know that the police and government are working hard to keep us all safe.

Question: I saw these kids in some country, maybe Afghanistan, all maimed by bombs. They said it was from our soldiers. Why do our soldiers hurt kids? I thought Canadian soldiers were peacekeepers. (From a boy in Grade 6)
Response: Canadian soldiers are trying to help build up the country and provide security, so if what you saw was correct, all I can think is that maybe the children were injured by land mines. No one wants to hurt anyone, especially children, but sometimes there are unintended casualties. Those children have families just like we do, and parents who worry about them too. The soldiers have jobs to do, but they don't want to hurt children.

Question: I saw bombs exploding on TV. Will we get bombed? Or what about Toronto or Vancouver? (From a girl in Grade 4)
Response: No, I'm quite sure we won't. The bombs you saw were probably in Iraq or Afghanistan — far from here. Our government and police are working to prevent anything like that happening.

Good Idea

Use something like the question about terrorists and response about violence as an opening to discuss alternative ways to handle differences and resolve conflicts.

Good Idea

Adopt a question such as the one from the Grade 5 boy about the traditional dress of the man wearing a turban to discuss and debunk stereotyping and racial biases. See also the margin note on page 41.

Good Idea

Keep a globe or large world map on a wall in your room to locate the countries mentioned so that students can get an idea of how far away they are.

Question: I saw the news on television and this guy said that Yemen was a hot spot of fighting and that the government couldn't control it. He sounded scared. Could that fighting come here too? Why couldn't the government do anything? (From a girl in Grade 6)

Response: Yemen is a trouble spot right now and it's frightening when we think of fighting anywhere. Possibly, he meant that the government wasn't effective right now, but we must remember that all governments are working hard to stop fighting everywhere. Remember that Canada is a peace-keeping country. I don't believe that the fighting you are referring to could ever somehow spread to here.

Question: What's a smart bomb? (From a boy in Grade 3)

Response: What do you know about them already?

Reply: I think they can follow a target like in James Bond movies. That's really scary because someone, say, in Iraq could send a bomb here to get us.

Response: You are mostly right. A smart bomb can be directed to some extent, that's what makes it "smart." But there is no reason for our city to be bombed. We are not at war.

Question: Why is there war anyway? Why do we have to kill other people? (From a girl in Grade 4)

Response: That's a good question. War is frightening for everyone. Some people choose different ways to deal with problems, and they think differently than we do. Choosing to use violence to solve problems isn't good for anyone. That's why our government works to keep peace.

Question: I was watching a TV news show with my mom and it was all about this suicide bomber who killed a bunch of people in Afghanistan. And it was a *kid* who had all those bombs on him. Why would someone do that? (From a girl in Grade 5)

Response: What do you know about suicide bombers?

Reply: My mom told me. They kill themselves so that they can kill others. But I can't figure out why they'd do that.

Response: It is hard to understand why anyone would take their own life, as well as the lives of others they don't even know. The kids or others who agree to do that have been convinced it is the right thing to do. They've been lied to and sometimes told that their families would be paid after it was over. They have interpreted their religion to believe that what they are doing will be good for the world. Politics may also be involved. We may never really understand why they acted the way they did.

A final word to new-age teachers

When all is said and done, at the end of each day in the classroom, you must applaud yourself for doing the best you can do. You are a teacher, a role model, a mentor. There is no greater calling. But there is a single question you can ask yourself as you shut your classroom door every day: "Did I teach with passion and a hint of magic today?" I feel sure that most of the time, the answer will be "yes." On the occasional day when you answer with a "no," then you have another day, tomorrow, to be better.

Good Ideas

1. Have students find out how their community and school work to "keep the peace." Ask students what they can do to help maintain a peaceful community. (They can work to stop bullying, offer assistance to people in need, and so on.)
2. Create charts illustrating all the positive ways to handle conflicts. Post the charts where everyone can see them.

CHAPTER 6

Concerning 2010 + Schools

"In schools the main problem is not the absence of innovations but the presence of too many disconnected . . . piecemeal, superficially adorned projects. We are in over our heads."

— Michael Fullan

People aren't the only ones suffering from our current troubled times; many schools are being forced to take upsetting backward steps as well. Franklin Roosevelt said, "The school is the last expenditure upon which America should be willing to economize." He would not be happy with what's happening today. Blamed on the failing economy, school budget cuts mean bigger classes, less money for books and supplies, fewer teachers' aides, and ultimately, less help for students. All this at a time when the world is in such chaos that now more than ever we need well-educated students who can deal with and resolve tomorrow's problems.

Today is not a good time to cut back funds to education. Indeed, there is never a good time to cut these funds, but when we consider the mess we have made of the 2010 world, we should be pouring every cent along with the best ever teachers into the education of our youth. We can't, unfortunately, control the money, but I know we have better teachers than ever before. I hope that this chapter of *Teaching in Troubled Times* will help teachers become even better by addressing some school-related issues that cause them distress.

Teachers today need courage. Theirs is not an easy career at the best of times, and if one considers today as being more like the "worst of times," then their lot in life seems precarious. Teachers are, however, our best resource for making the future better than it is today. They hold the keys to tomorrow's success, so if you are a teacher who's reading this (and who else would be reading it?), you are probably feeling the stress. Good. That stress will give you courage, and this book will give you ideas for helping your school "be better." There are things you can do with minimum effort and time on your part and no money. These measures include improving school spirit, involving the community, updating school philosophy and mission statements, and working within the confines of a budget that does not allow for enough current textbooks.

School Spirit in Troubled Times

One big problem with economic cutbacks to schools has nothing to do with the tightness of money, but with teachers' reactions to that. Teachers all know what happens when a new, tight budget is revealed. As a teacher myself, I know that we groan, complain, and as a group work ourselves into a state of near panic: "How can I teach math with only enough texts for half the class?" Sure, that's going to be tough, but it is what it is, and all the complaining will not make the situation better. So, let's think "school spirit" and adopt a different attitude because teachers' attitudes are instantly reflected in students' attitudes. The following are suggestions for improving school spirit regardless of how tough times are, beginning with a share-with-the-school Formula Five.

Be "everywhere" positive.
Be in-school creative.
Be colleague supportive.
Encompass your community.
Be internally interactive.

For more school spirit ideas than can ever be used, go to this Web site: http://wacaonline.org/resources-spirit.

Formula Five: Encouraging School Spirit

Be "everywhere" positive. It's just as easy to think, speak, and act positively as it is to behave negatively; in fact, "positivity" takes considerably less energy than "negativity." Refuse to say anything negative about your school either in school or away from it, and refuse to accept that from your students or colleagues. The following is a fun way to keep positivity in focus.

- *Punch Me, Please:* Put simply, you give permission to colleagues to punch you (lightly and in the arm, please) whenever you say anything negative or act in any way detrimental to positive school spirit. This works well when the entire staff buys into it and treats it "gently" as a way to constantly remind one another to stay positive. I have used the same technique with my significant other when, at home, I've started to "whine" and express negative thoughts about my school (these thoughts only make me feel worse about the situation and are never productive). My husband loved punching me in the arm when this happened, and he was much less gentle than colleagues at school.

Be in-school creative. With colleagues and students, brainstorm creative ways to punch up school spirit. The following is an example.

- *True-to-You, _____* [The blank is for the name of your school.]: When times are troubled, as they are at the beginning of this new decade, it's easy to blame someone, something, some place. School shortages (whether they be supplies or staff) cause distress, and the blame tends to fall on the school itself. "This school is terrible — there's not even enough paper towels." "The discipline at this school is really poor." "Staff here are all so moody." So, the first suggestion is to incorporate "Punch Me, Please" into your staff room, then follow that quickly with suggestions for "True-to-You" activities, whole-school activities that promote school pride and school spirit.

  The old adage "When times are tough, the tough get going" is true here. Few things are more powerful than an optimistic attitude, and that's what is needed when you find yourself or your colleagues, or even the students, berating the school. You must get everyone involved in creative spirit activities, such as generating school songs or chants, having a fund-raising challenge, holding a themed rally (e.g., Wild, Wild West fitness rally), promoting a spirit contest where students come up with the ideas, crafting a teacher baby-pictures contest or a class bubble-gum blowing contest (each class chooses one contestant), starting door decorating contests, fashioning a school mascot (e.g., a superhero named and dressed appropriately as the Mapleridge X-Man — "The X-Man can!").

Be colleague supportive. When times are tough, it's easy to get caught up in our own worries and forget that we are part of a team. Make time to help colleagues be positive, feel good about the school, appreciate their positions, and consequently, boost school spirit. There are many subtle little ways to do this, including turning negative statements into positive ones. For example, take "I'm so fed up with how cold my classroom is." That statement could become "I agree the heating system isn't good, but I'm so glad to have a job that I just keep a bunch of sweaters at my desk. Maybe we should have a "sweater day" and have kids all wear their brightest sweaters?" Another idea is to involve everyone in the "Buddy Bonus" (see page 108).

User-Friendly Volunteers is the term I use to signify making the best possible use of volunteers with the minimum of effort. See the discussion below.

The following is a suggestion for supporting peers who tend to be negative and for helping them to see things more positively.

- *Five-Day Favors:* Each day for one week, do something positive for a troubled peer. To be most effective, do it anonymously and secretly. The bonus is that it works as a wonderful pick-me-up for the giver, you, as well as for the receiver. The little acts might include a special coffee or muffin or pastry on his desk in the morning, doing his staff-room cleanup for one day, cleaning his mail slot of the junk that seems to multiply there, tidying his desk after school, and leaving a funny note or joke attached to his computer. On the fifth day (a Friday probably), add a note to the offering saying something like "The positives this week have come from the Think-Positive Pixie. Be well." It's amazing how this simple activity reduces personal disquiet and enhances school spirit.

Encompass your community. Keep lines of communication open within the school community — the businesses, community leagues, apartment complexes, and homes adjacent to the school. There are many good reasons for this, such as the pulling of user-friendly volunteers (page 112), canvassing for fund raisers, and seeking of donations for activities such as the school barbeque or track and field days, all of which increase overall school spirit. Community communication can be managed by posting upcoming school activity posters (made by students); delivering formal invitations to community members (not just to parents) to attend school activities, such as concerts, athletic endeavors, open houses, and such; or writing letters to community businesses. I know you can think of many other ways to achieve community communication; the following example works especially well in today's "think-green" world.

- *Clean-Green Community:* Boost school morale as well as community relations with a community cleanup done by the school. Use area maps and assign each class one section of the community adjacent to the school to clean. Pick a day, inform the community, provide garbage bags and plastic gloves, involve volunteers to help supervise, and get moving. Finish off with a barbeque in the schoolyard (perhaps sponsored by community businesses that will probably be very willing under the circumstances) or even just a drink-and-snacks time. This activity is super for school spirit.

Be internally interactive. School spirit is only as strong as the school's teachers are happy and positive, so anything that can boost teachers' joy in teaching within the school day will naturally boost school spirit. Here are two suggestions that help to accomplish this.

- *Staff Meeting Magic:* Okay, so all staff meetings are boring and time consuming and seem to drag on and leave you with headaches, but what if you could leave each one with a single, exciting, fun idea or tip that you could use in your class the next day? Early in the year, teachers draw months randomly and are responsible for bringing to the meeting of their month a novel idea for a motivator (see pages 94–102), an interesting idea, a teaching tip . . . whatever can be quickly shared. The presentation must take no more than five minutes and must be something everyone can use. For instance, you could share the motivator "Scribble Sense" (page 95) and let teachers try it. What fun! What a good way to end a staff meeting.
- *Mission Re-do:* Ask the principal to bring the school philosophy or mission statement to a staff meeting. Most of these were probably written some time

ago, and given the current state of affairs and changing curriculum, need revising. Refer to the hints given about personal philosophies (pages 93–94) and as a group, "modernize" that statement. This exercise tends to give school spirit a shot in the arm, especially if the whole document is made short and more meaningful.

Dealing with School-Related Shortages

A real problem that is a direct result of today's foundering economy is the financial cutbacks to education and to schools, with the resulting shortages of paper, supplies, books, support staff, even teachers.

In one school the shortages were even reflected in toilet tissue. Although the issue was rather a source of amusement, a local supermarket became involved and donated a mountain of tissue which, in turn, began a fortuitous, mutually beneficial arrangement between the supermarket and the school. Of course, this shortage was the result of an oversight; schools really don't run out of basic necessities. But the incident does draw attention to today's school shortages — and teachers are the ones who have to figure out what to do about them. I love this quotation by Haim G. Ginott: "Teachers are expected to reach unattainable goals with inadequate tools. The miracle is that at times they accomplish this impossible task."

Complaining about all the things we think we need to make us better teachers is a waste of time and energy that could be better spent employing one of the suggestions below. I realize it's easy for me to say "do this, do that" and much more difficult for the classroom teacher to do it, but if the teacher is already struggling with shortages of supplies, then he or she will be less troubled by trying one of the strategies, all of which have been generously shared with me by teachers who are also struggling.

Community school closures

Another disturbing "shortage" that is all too rapidly emerging is that of community schools: in some jurisdictions, boards of education are slating schools for closure or putting them at risk of being closed. This phenomenon is directly tied to the failing economy. School boards need a minimum number of students registered at a school to make it financially feasible to keep it operating, and with neighborhoods changing and budgets being cut, boards are making tough decisions in tough times. Students, teachers, and parents, however, don't view this frustrating situation from the economical point of view. To them it is a catastrophe, demoralizing and emotion packed. As a rule, even when parents come together to fight for a community school, schools slated for closure close. If not immediately, then sometime soon.

This situation is highly heated, exasperating, and emotional for all involved, but since it is largely between parents and school boards, there is not much teachers can do. Yet I don't mean to suggest that teachers are not involved. They are. With this in mind I offer the following suggestions for teachers who must deal with the closure of the school at which they teach.

- Remain as positive as possible, keeping in mind that parents and students will mimic your attitude, and a negative attitude won't solve anything.
- Be willing to get involved in, or at least be visible at, school board meetings, community meetings, and parent meetings. Show your support for the

existing school, but be as open-minded as possible — in other words, remember that you work for the school board and don't want to jeopardize your position by being overly radical.

- Talk to students about choices, about where else they will be able to get excellent educations, and emphasize the positive points about those schools.
- Be supportive of parents by letting them know about other great schools and what they have to offer. Try to reassure parents that their children's education will not suffer as a result of the school closure; ideally, there will be measures taken to improve it.
- Arrange for parents and students to visit neighboring schools where the children may go. Work with the host schools who will probably "put their best faces forward."
- Invite the parents of your students to a class meeting where they can freely air their concerns. If possible, have your principal together with a school board member at the meeting and even a teacher from a school to which the students might go in the future. A small, single-class meeting lets parents feel they are not alone.
- For yourself, remember that change can be positive, and even if you have taught at this school for many wonderful years, you will likely have just as positive an experience at a new school if you allow yourself to remain positive.

Shortages of textbooks

I have collected several options for this dilemma. Each option allows not only for textbook shortages, but also promotes positive learning of some sort.

Split the class.
Adopt the buddy system.
Take a reference-text approach.
Partner a purchase.
Prepare group presentations.

Formula Five: Dealing with Textbook Shortages

Split the class. Each half uses the texts on alternate days. When not using the text, the other half is involved in review activities from an overhead or board — that's thinking green. This approach promotes independent work because the teacher works with one group at a time.

Adopt the buddy system. There is one text per pair: each buddy is allowed to "own the text" (take it home if so desired) on alternate weeks or days. If it's *A*'s turn to own, but he doesn't need it, *B* can ask for permission to own it that night and so on. This system promotes sharing and responsibility; in some cases, it can also promote peer tutoring.

Take a reference-text approach. When there are only 2 or 3 textbooks, keep one for reference; the other two are placed in the class reading centre, not to be removed from the class. Use your copy to choose the most important parts that will be delivered in lessons, on overheads, on the board, or, as a last resort, on photocopies. This approach promotes the almost lost skills of copying (from overhead, board), listening (to your lessons), and taking jot notes, or quick points from lectures.

Partner a purchase. Partner with another class in the school or from a neighboring school that has the same shortages as you. Between the two schools you may be able to purchase a single class set and create a sharing arrangement so that both schools have use of the set at different times. Arranging this is a great job for user-friendly volunteers (see page 112) and fosters connections with a peer school.

Prepare group presentations. If only a few textbooks are available, small groups working together can prepare presentations of the salient points as outlined by you. In this case each group can have the use of a single textbook, or different groups can use different texts. Group effort promotes the development of communication, research, and writing skills.

Lack of relevancy of available textbooks

It seems that the curriculum is never stable; a new series of texts is barely in the classrooms than the curriculum changes again, making very expensive books quickly redundant. First, let me remind you of what you already know. No matter how pretty, clean, and shiny those new texts are, the old ones probably contain almost identical material and should not be discarded. Schools today cannot afford to keep up with the big publishing companies who fight for contracts to provide the latest in glossy textbooks at a high cost to themselves and to schools. So, given that you are using "old" textbooks, try to supplement with one or two of the new ones, just for teacher resources; then, use the "reference text" or "group presentation" approaches suggested above to cover only the material that does not appear in the earlier books.

Here are a few other ideas:

- Purchase only the Teachers' Guide for the new series. It will give you all you need to know about what is not covered by whatever references you have.
- Supplement "old texts" with Internet research based on what still needs to be covered, or with magazine or newspaper articles. These are often even more up-to-date than the new texts.
- Have older students who need a challenge (as expressed by their teachers) skim the old and new texts to locate and document differences, and make sure you check the latest curriculum content yourself to find similar differences. Doing this is your professional responsibility. You can thereby avoid spending time on topics no longer deemed necessary and will know exactly what appears only in the new books. User-friendly volunteers can help make comparisons too (see page 112).

Shortages of paper, writing tools, and art supplies

Shortage of supplies, too, is a very real concern for teachers today. The computer age was supposed to lessen our need for paper — that hasn't happened. And paper is expensive. Teachers today frequently find themselves rationing paper, attempting to stay within the limiting confines of the number of pages per teacher per month allotment. The same problem arises with general supplies, such as paperclips, pencils, art supplies, science supplies, health supplies . . . basically an inadequate supply of consumable materials. Schools are forced to cut corners drastically; too often that responsibility is passed on to the classroom teachers. One teacher jokingly told me she had an entire museum display right in her classroom — her classroom computers. Certainly, considerable teacher stress is centred on financial constraints and lack of educational supplies. Too often, teachers pay out of their pockets for some of the basic necessities, causing more stress to their own financial situations.

So, what can be done to help with this situation? First, you have to face the fact that as teachers you can't control how much money you are allotted; then, you have to creatively find alternatives. In the past, parents could often be counted on to help purchase supplies for their offspring, but in today's tough economy, that is no longer possible for many; it is unfair to have some students with more supplies than they need, while others have none. Here are some suggestions, presented in a Formula Five:

Formula Five: "Found" Classroom Supplies

Seek community assistance. Community ventures, frequently based in a community league building that has a president, secretary, and board members, may be willing to fund-raise or give donations to a specific class or school for the purchase of supplies. For example, everyone in the community where I live is provided regularly with flyers telling when community meetings are to be held, who the members of office are and so forth. It is easy to contact any of these people at any time. If your school has done a good job of community public relations, then approaching members of the community for help may be easier. Be sure to know exactly what is needed — for example, $200 for art supplies — when you approach a possible donor. Use the initiative as a total learning experience for the students, involving them in letter writing and interviewing.

Take the class conservation challenge. Challenge the students to think of ways to save paper. Gone are the days of writing a couple of lines on a page, crumpling it up, and discarding it. Teach the kids to "use every scrap." Share with them the true tale of the youngster from Cuba who had a single sheet of paper on which to write so he wrote so very small and on every corner and in every direction that only he could read it. The paper was parchment thin and heavily wrinkled, but it was his pride and joy. A few ideas are writing smaller but still legibly, using erasers instead of scribbling out, using both sides of paper, and using inexpensive newsprint for planning and working out problems and such. One student suggested asking the school secretary to save any "used pages that still had room to write" for them. The secretary, who checked for "privacy" of used pages, supplied the class with enough "rough pages" for an entire year's worth of problem solving, doodling, and planning.

Similarly, students can be challenged to use pencils until they are too short to hold, to be economical as opposed to wasteful with coloring materials — basically, to begin to appreciate the value of all those items that for so long have been taken for granted. Modeling is important here. Be sure that you are getting the absolute most out of a page. I will never forget the Grade 3 student who said loudly and clearly, "Teacher, you have left all the bottom of this page blank [photocopied math problems] and that's just not acceptable."

Shift gears to reverse. Instead of relying heavily on photocopied materials which can become very costly and paper inefficient, resort to older methods of teaching that truly work just as well for many subjects. Use overhead projectors with erasable pen notes for problems or information for students to copy, work out, or read. Remember how teachers once wrote copious notes on the boards? Try returning to this method occasionally to save paper. While you will still expect students to copy notes to their own pages, you will quickly rediscover how much you abbreviate and stick to key points only when writing on the board.

Visit an office supply store. Most towns and certainly all cities have large office supply outlets or stores, such as Staples or Office Depot. Visit one (preferably with a couple of students in tow), and ask for donations by explaining the benefits to the store. These include tax write-offs, community public relations, and free advertising (you will let parents know where the supplies came from). You might even invite representatives from the store to your class to see their product in use; for example, they could watch an art class. These types of stores are seldom pursued for hand-outs like these, so you just might find them supportive.

Double-up. Have students work together sharing supplies, such as paints, colored pencils, and so on. If possible, establish these partnerships at the outset of the year so that students will not have to purchase as much (one student buys colored pencils; the other buys water paints). In that way, you will benefit parents also. Be a good model: arrange to share supplies such as audio-visual materials with another teacher.

Maintaining a Positive Classroom

The school may be old and tired, the washrooms cold and drafty, the staff room cramped and uncomfortable, but in your room, you are the king or the queen in your private castle. Read the wise words of Tracy Kidder: "Most teachers have little control over school policy or curriculum or choice of texts or special placement of students, but most have a great deal of autonomy inside the classroom. To a degree shared by only a few other occupations, such as police work, public education rests precariously on the skill and virtue of the people at the bottom of the institutional pyramid." How true. Teachers have complete control once their classroom doors are shut. What a huge responsibility! What an enormous honor! So, regardless of the troubled times in which we live, regardless of the lack of money for education or the shortages experienced in your school, close your door and smile. Make your class a happy, caring, fun-filled place that promotes real learning and where students want to be taught. You know how to do this, but I would remind you (as I always remind myself) to use the following Formula Five consistently. Of course, there are many other ways to maintain a positive classroom, but the five below may be the most important.

Motivate.
Maintain simplicity.
Have fun.
Be realistic.
Enjoy time with each student.

Formula Five: Responsibilities of the Room "King" or "Queen"

Motivate. Always keep in mind that not all students want to be there, and not all students are motivated to learn. Motivating them is a professional responsibility, so, think in terms of quick motivators and ask yourself: "What turns the kids on?" "How can I capture their attention before I begin?" "How can I keep them interested?" Basically — think like a kid!

Maintain simplicity. Avoid the temptation to be too complicated in anything, including these areas:

- room decorations (Less is best here: An over-cluttered room is distracting to many kids.)
- lessons (Take baby steps.)
- expectations (Expect good work, but expect it one step at a time.)
- rules (Three or four classroom rules will be remembered and respected, while a dozen will be forgotten.)

Keep it simple, please.

Have fun. Teaching is fun. It is joyous. Oh, not all the time; I know there are "those days" and I appreciate the pressures of the job, but on the whole, teaching is fun if you allow it to be. Remind yourself that if it becomes "never fun," it's time to take action. That may mean introducing a motivator or game, taking a teacher time-out (see "Recharging Teacher's Batteries . . . ," pages 108–13), or just taking a break as a class and doing something fun together. Keep that sense of humor well fed and healthy.

Be realistic. If things go wrong with a lesson, don't fuss. Remind yourself that you are in your castle, that you are in control, and that there is something to be learned from every botched lesson or silly mistake. You might even share this "learning" with the students: "I wanted you to learn . . . from this lesson, but I think all that happened was that I learned this wasn't the way to teach it. Boy, did I mess up!" Again, what you teach is not so important as who you are. Students learn so much more from you as a person, an individual, a mentor, a *real* person who makes mistakes than from what you teach.

Enjoy time with each student. Make a promise to yourself to spend at least a few minutes one-to-one with every child every week. Do this in a way that works for you, and make certain you take the time. One example might be the open talk time, suggested on page 32. Another might be inviting students to "visit" you one at a time while you sit at a table at the back of the classroom. This special time is extremely important for the students and for you.

It would be interesting to look into the future and see how schools will have changed. Some soothsayers predict that schools in the next few decades will no longer be needed, that they are a tired and worn-out institution. They say that with the advancements in technology, all children will eventually be taught by robots and computers, making schools and teachers obsolete. They are wrong! Our children will always need the compassion, socialization, and nurturing they receive from teachers in schools, and whether these are modern, windowless, technology-laden constructions or old, brick buildings with worn-out desks and the occasional chalkboard, schools will always be important to education.

There will, of course, be changes. Schools will challenge, and accept, the evolution of technology. Teachers will become better facilitators, and teaching and learning will become interchangeable. Schools, teachers, parents, and even styles of learning will all change, but each will remain integral to the growth and development of future generations. Children will change, too; their expectations of and for education will keep pace with the constantly shifting technology. Tomorrow's students will probably not be satisfied with sit-and-listen types of traditional teaching approaches. They will expect, and deserve, education to be as exciting as the world in which they live. Technology for them will provide a continuous learning environment, and teachers will facilitate this. In the future, innovative teachers and compassionate, contemporary schools will teach, socialize, support, and protect children, just as they do now.

These are troubled times. Adults are troubled. Children are troubled. The world is troubled. But one almost trouble-free place remains for children: their school. Let us work to keep it that way and remember, as B. B. King put it, "The beautiful thing about learning is that no one can take it away from you."

Index